Perseverance

Understanding Sexual Violence

WENDY DONALDSON

authorHOUSE®

AuthorHouse™
1663 Liberty Drive
Bloomington, IN 47403
www.authorhouse.com
Phone: 1-800-839-8640

First published by AuthorHouse 3/29/2011

ISBN: 978-1-4567-3695-8 (e)
ISBN: 978-1-4567-3696-5 (sc)

Library of Congress Control Number: 2011902390

Printed in the United States of America

Any people depicted in stock imagery provided by Thinkstock are models,
and such images are being used for illustrative purposes only.
Certain stock imagery © Thinkstock.

This book is printed on acid-free paper.

Dedication

To Joye Cook and Greg Bolin;
I wish every survivor were as blessed as I to have such care.

To Cyndi Thornton;
You're always full of hope and optimism, and
the best friend a friend could have.

"All that is required for the triumph of evil is that good people remain silent and do nothing."

~Sir Edmond Burke

Acknowledgements

There were many people who have helped make this book possible. First of all, I would like to thank the Rape, Abuse, and Incest National Network (RAINN) for all they do in aiding, directing, and educating those affected by all forms of sexual violence. By having one of the most comprehensively thorough collections of information available on their website, they are making a huge impact on how victims come to terms, heal, and then become survivors. I would like to extend a huge thanks to Joye Cook for sharing her knowledge from over 23 years of working with victims of sex crimes. This world is a far better place by simply having her in it. I would also like to say thanks to Greg Bolin for his opinions, advise, and continued support over the years. Even after 30 years in law enforcement (and still going strong), your dedicated service is truly appreciated, and your considerate experience is certainly a benefit to your field. And a big thanks to Cyndi Thornton for making sure I stay on my toes and have all my ducks in a row. I would especially like to thank all of the volunteer groups & organizations that strive to help guide and educate victims of sexual violence. Your hard work and dedication is appreciated more than you'll ever know. And last, but certainly not least, I want to thank my entire family for all of their unwavering support and understanding. I am truly blessed to have each and every one of you.

Table of Contents

My Survival Story

July 13, 1991 – Southern Arkansas

As many teenagers do, I told my mother that I was spending the night with a friend and wouldn't return home until the next afternoon. In reality, I wanted to go to a party with my boyfriend, at the time, and I didn't want a curfew. A few of my friends were telling their parents the same thing so that we could all stay out late, together. This party was way out in the country where the noise wouldn't bother anyone. There seemed to be about 30-40 people there by the time we arrived, but there were car loads coming and going all through the night. Everyone either had a beer from the keg or some mixed concoction that someone had brought with them. As usual, when you mix adolescents and alcohol, bad judgment is bound to occur. It had to be a little past one in the morning when I got into an argument with my boyfriend. Even during the argument, I noticed this guy, wearing a florescent green baseball cap, staring at me. At the time I thought he was just wondering why I was crying. He did look a little older than the other people out there, since most at the party were in their late teens and early 20's. I then heard one of my friends suggest that I go for a walk to calm down. Immediately the guy wearing the bright green baseball cap came over and said that he would go along,

1

so that I wouldn't be alone. He introduced himself and said that he was friends with my boyfriend. I do remember thinking *"I don't even know this guy,"* but he looked normal enough, so I dismissed that thought as being paranoid, my first of a few mistakes to come.

As we walked down the dark country road he kept passing me some mixed drink that he was carrying, telling me to "drink up!" After the first sip, I realized that I didn't like it. Once I refused the next offer, he quickly downed the rest of the drink and threw the empty cup into the woods. I remember him coming across awfully anxious as we walked. It seemed that the further we walked, the more nervous I began to feel. Even though he claimed to be friends with my boyfriend, many of his comments were so off base that I began to wonder if he even knew him. Then this guy mentioned that he dated my boyfriend's sister, and that's when I knew that something wasn't right, because his sister was only 13 years old and didn't date. That was when I noticed that we had actually walked farther from the party than I had realized. I could no longer hear the music and chatter from the crowd we left behind. As soon as I mentioned that I was ready to go back to the party, he stepped in front of me and kissed me. Pressing my hands against his chest, I pushed him away and told him again that I wanted to go back. He turned away so quickly that it was obvious he was angry. After he took only a couple of steps, he spun back around and punched me right between the eyes. The sudden white burst of lights and ringing in my ears stunned me for a moment, but as it began to sink in what was actually happening, he threw another punch. After the third blow to my face, he grabbed me by my hair, drug me across the ditch, then into the thick, dark woods. At first, I remember thinking that I could talk my way out of what was about to happen, but with each attempt the beating only got worse. I suppose his logic was if I was knocked out, then I couldn't fight him.

This is where I remember only segments, after losing and then regaining consciousness several times. When I finally did regain consciousness, my face was in the ground and I could feel him behind me. Along with the realization of what he was doing to me, I suddenly felt a wave of nausea. I could tell that my shirt was gone, and I could feel the sticks and thorns beneath me being ground into my stomach and chest with his every thrust. I could also feel my jeans near my ankles, restricted by the lace-up boots that I was wearing. This made it feel as though my ankles were bound together. When I raised my head to try to look in front of me, I could see the headlights of a car passing on the road just a short distance in front of us. But before I could even get a breath, I felt a cloth coming over my head. I was only able to get my fingertips under the cloth just before he tightened it around the front of my neck. As he pulled back on the cloth wrapped around my throat, he pressed in the center of my back with his knee. I could feel my airway closing, and the burning in my chest from lack of air. Then came his voice from behind me saying *"Damn bitch, die!"* That statement alone removed any doubt that I had about him killing me. As my lungs felt as though they were on fire, I thought *"I'm going to die out here and no one will ever find me."* As soon as he gave up on choking me, he rolled me over to face him. I felt so relieved that I could finally breathe again, that I didn't even wonder why he wanted me to face him. Immediately he grabbed a handful of hair on the right side of my head and began to punch the left side of my face repeatedly, until I was once again unconscious.

The next time I woke, I could see sunlight peeking through the trees. Then I suddenly remembered why I was laying on the ground in these woods. Looking around, I could see that I was alone. But I also noticed that I couldn't open one of my eyes, and that moving my neck was a major challenge for some reason. Then I realized that I couldn't feel anything at all; complete and total numbness. I started raising my hands in front of my face; since I wasn't able to look down to survey the damage. My hands, wrists and arms were covered in trails of dried blood. I suddenly felt a desperate need to find where the blood had come from. I reached for my neck to find that it was so swollen that it was almost even with my jaw line. I could feel more trails of dried blood as I felt around my ears. But as soon as I touched the eye that wouldn't open, I quickly understood why. My left eye was so swollen that I couldn't even pry it open with my fingers. Trying to reign in some of the panic, I attempted to see if I was hurt anywhere else. As I felt over my chest, I only found my torn bra scarcely covering part of my chest. Reaching lower, I found my jeans bunched up near my ankles. As I tried to pull my jeans back up, I realized that I could only get them about halfway over my hips. Something was preventing them from fitting right, but I couldn't tell what it was, and I still couldn't feel anything. Since the zipper also felt ripped, I could only hold them up as best I could. I knew that I had to find help fast. Leaving the woods, I climbed over the ditch and onto the road.

I'm not sure why I started walking towards the west, especially considering that there was an Interstate less than a mile to the east. Thankfully I awoke when I did and began walking west. Not seeing any cars or houses in front of me, I turned to look behind me and froze in the middle of the road. Suddenly, I couldn't breathe; I couldn't even move for a moment. All of my focus was on the florescent green cap that I could see glowing in the sun just a little ways behind me. All I could think was *"now he's really going to kill me!"* I forced myself to turn around and tried to run away. Soon I realized that I was moving in slow motion compared to the effort it took to try to run. Something was making it very difficult to move my legs correctly, but I couldn't look down to see why. Before long, I thought I heard a vehicle coming from behind me. Looking back, I saw a car driving towards me, and the bright green cap was no where in sight. As the car pulls up next to me, I see an older man, with thinning hair and glasses, driving the car. I quickly told this man about the guy out there who was trying to kill me and how desperately I needed his help. I'll never forget the look on his face, right before telling me that he didn't want to get involved. Despite all my begging and pleading, he slowly pulled away, and drove west, and out of sight. I just stood there, stunned. It was so hard for me to believe that he just left me there to be killed. Then, I thought to look behind me again. Sure enough, there was that gleaming green cap once again, coming out of the tree line and moving towards me. Suddenly, I was kind of glad that he was wearing that bright colored cap, if only so that I could better see exactly where he was. I knew that my only hope was to keep moving west, trying to stay as far ahead of him as possible. When I did look back, I could see that he was getting closer. He was obviously moving faster than me, being that he wasn't the injured person. I just kept telling myself "MOVE, MOVE, MOVE!" Instead of looking back, I tried to solely focus on putting one foot in front of the other. It couldn't have been much longer before I thought I heard another car coming from behind. When I looked back this time, I saw a car approaching and that neon green cap had vanished again. I knew then that he was only hiding at the edge of the woods, watching to see if anyone would help me. I was determined not to let this car simply pass me by. While holding my torn bra as best I could with one hand, I used the other to hold my jeans at my hips, and planted myself right in the middle of the road. Once the car stopped, I could see a young woman was driving with a male passenger. It didn't take much pleading before the woman was helping me into the back of her car. She told me that she saw a guy wearing a florescent green cap stoop into the woods as they approached the area where he was. She then said that they looked a little further down the road and saw me walking down a hill. I vaguely remember the ride back to her house where she called 911. Before blacking out again, I do remember the guy in the car ripping the neckband of his t-shirt so it would fit over my head without restricting my neck. I suppose that I felt safer knowing that I had found someone who was actually trying to help me.

I next woke in the Trauma Center of the local hospital hearing voices all around me. I specifically heard a male voice saying the words 'possible broken facial bones', and then another say that immediate surgery was needed. That alone is enough to send a teenage girl into a state of panic. As I opened my good eye, I saw a couple of white coats standing around me. Then I saw a sturdy build lady sitting in a chair to my right. She stated that she was with the local rape crisis center, and that she would stay with me. She kept repeating that I was safe now and had nothing to fear. I remember trying to speak, but my mouth felt like it was glued shut it was so dry. I just assumed that the surgery they said I needed was for my face. That is until I woke much later in a recovery room and learned that I had to have a 5-hour reconstructive surgery for my vaginal and anal areas. Even the rape kit had to be completed in the operating room. I was told that the surgeon believed that I had been sodomized by a small tree limb, evident by the amount of tree bark that had to be removed internally. At that age, I had no idea as to what sodomy even meant. It was explained to me that, at some point during the attack, the guy had ripped out some of my insides with a small tree branch. This made me realize that the ripped internal tissue hanging out of me was the reason I couldn't pull my jeans all the way up, and why I couldn't get my legs to work correctly when I was trying to run away. This surgeon also told me that the damage could have been a lot worse if that guy had been able to free even one leg from my boots and tapered leg jeans. When I asked about the number of stitches, he said that they had just stopped counting after 200. I especially hated hearing that, due to the amount of damaged internal tissue, it would now, in all probability, be very difficult for me to have children.

It only took the sheriff's department a couple of hours to find the guy who attacked me. Once I was rescued, he apparently went running east through the woods, in the opposite direction. There was one resident who reported that she woke early to find a guy, wearing a bright green baseball cap, pulling an ax head from her storage building behind her house. Then a different neighbor had called the sheriffs office about a guy, with that same description, trying to hot-wire a truck in her front yard. Then, yet another area resident woke to a guy knocking on his door, which looked rather anxious and covered in debris, asking to use the phone. He even used his real name. These calls lead deputies to an area about a mile or two to the east of where I was rescued. Deputies found my attacker on a nearby highway trying to get away on a stolen bicycle. After getting a positive ID on him from the lady whose truck he tried to hot-wire, they then took him to the county jail, where he asked for his attorney.

Once I was moved into a private room, I noticed that everything in the room that reflected was covered. Even the mirrors had white sheets sealed over them with surgical tape. This made me think *"I must look pretty bad if no one wants me to see myself."* My fear of what I would see was much stronger than my curiosity at that time. I had enough to focus on, between convincing myself where I was whenever I woke and the visitors that came. It seemed a different nurse came into the room every couple of hours, but all of them were so attentive, and also dreadfully sympathetic. I wasn't sure just how many more times I could stand to hear *"I'm so sorry this happened to you."* I understood that they meant well, and that that was the appropriate thing to say, but it also seemed to serve as an instant reminder of what I had survived. I even woke a couple of times to find my father sitting in a chair next to my bed silently crying. Once, I pretended to be asleep when he looked up at me. I just felt too ashamed of what had happened to face him at that moment. I remember wondering if I had dreamed or imagined that sturdy-built lady from the rape crisis center, because I hadn't seen or heard from her since before my surgery. I was visited a few times by the criminal investigators with the local sheriff's department. The lead investigator, Greg Bolin, was so very supportive and tolerant. He made me feel that I could trust him, and that he truly was there to help me. During one visit, they had brought a card of Polaroid pictures of a bunch of guys, and I was able to point out the one who attacked me. He wasn't wearing that hideously neon green cap, but I could tell it was him. That was when I learned that I was his second victim within 104 days. It seems that he was out on bail from prior rape and kidnapping charges when he attacked, and tried to kill me. These veteran investigators also mentioned that this assault was one of the worst they had ever seen without being a homicide. They told me that the prior victim wanted nothing more than to forget that her attack had ever happened. She even told the police that she couldn't forget it if they keep bringing it up to her. I couldn't blame her really; I didn't want to remember it either. But one fact kept going through my mind. If I didn't cooperate and help with putting this guy away, then he would never stop! It would only be a matter of time before he did this to another girl. Many people believed that the next girl that he attacked would almost certainly not make it. It was quite obvious to everyone that he was getting worse with each physical attack.

After a couple of days in the hospital, I was released to go home. The CID investigators asked me to show them the exact spot where the assault had occurred. This proved to be far more difficult than I thought it would be. The thick woods along that road all looked the same. There were no specific markers I could follow, nothing that stood out in my mind except for the hill in the thinly paved road. I remembered how difficult it was trying to climb that little hill the next morning, so I knew that it had to be somewhere before that hill, and on the north side of the road. Regrettably, that was the best I could provide for the investigators as far as the exact spot where the attack happened. Being that it was a hot, humid, summer day, and that I had just had surgery a couple of days prior, I felt such a intense need to just rest for a couple of minutes. The sun seemed almost blinding it was so bright. Investigator Greg Bolin led me to his car so that I could sit in the air conditioning for a while. As soon as he went to open the passenger door of his car, I saw my reflection staring at me in the window. That was the first time I could get an idea as to just how different my face looked. The swelling, bruising and scratches were all horrifying. Greg swiftly caught my arms as my knees seemed to give out. All I could do was sit there and cry. I was extremely thankful to even be alive, but my face suddenly looked like some science experiment gone wrong. To me, my face and neck looked more like a balloon that had been over expanded. I couldn't help but wonder if I would ever look the same again.

Once I was back at home that afternoon, I felt such an irrepressible urge to see just how bad the damage to my face really was. My heart began to race as I walked down the hallway. Turning into the bathroom, I took a deep breath before flipping on the light switch. With that light came a sudden, sick feeling. It looked, to me, as if I weighed at least 100 pounds more just from the amount of inflammation. I could see that it was the left side of my face that took the brunt of the beatings. My neck was still very swollen, with faintly bruised impressions of my knuckles across the front. There were so many black and purple contusions covering much of my face. My chin, lips, left cheek and eye were as black as night. Then something else caught my attention. Looking closer in the mirror, I noticed that both of my eyeballs were completely red, as if all the vessels were busted. The person looking back at me looked like some kind of monster, something evil with blood red eyes. Maybe it was a little bit of vanity that had me so worried about my appearance and if I would ever look like I did before the attack, but that was a big concern for me. For years I had wanted so badly to become a fashion model. Looking into that mirror, all I could think was *"Who in the world would hire me as a model now?"* I felt as if anyone who looked at me would automatically know what had happened. Like some brand on cattle, stamped across my forehead… RAPED! No one is ever taught how to deal with something like that, at least not until it happens. About a dozen thoughts raced through my mind at once, but very little made much sense. I ran through all of the 'should've, could've, would've' scenarios until I felt that it was in some way my own fault. Maybe I should've ran as soon as I felt nervous about being alone with that guy; maybe I could've put up more of a fight, and maybe I wouldn't even be in this situation if I hadn't lied to my mother about where I was going that night. Guilt is a very heavy burden to carry, and I actually began to feel as though maybe this was God's punishment for my lying and sneaking.

While in the shower I began thinking about my internal injuries. Suddenly I couldn't shake the question, "*What could possibly make someone DO that to another human being?*" What could possess a person to actually use a small tree limb to mutilate a body? Then I started to wonder why I don't recall even a hint of a memory of that happening to me. How could I have survived that after, apparently, being completely defenseless? I could have just as easily died that night, alone in those dreadful woods; possibly never to have been found. Then I realized that this would be the first night I would sleep at home after the attack. I could tell the doctors had been generous with the pain medications during my stay in the hospital, because I was suddenly able to feel far too much. There was a throbbing pain shooting throughout the lower part of my body and a stiff soreness settled deeply in every muscle. I honestly thought that a hot shower and a couple of pain pills would get me through the night well enough. I soon learned that 'getting through the night' was far more difficult than I thought it would be. Every time I closed my eyes, I would see a florescent green baseball cap coming at me. Whenever I slept I would hear his voice echoing through my head, saying *"Damn bitch, die!"* Several mental images of that night seemed to be tattooed into my brain. The steady flow of night terrors and flashbacks became my own living hell for quite some time.

My attacker was prosecuted for his prior kidnapping

and rape charges, as well as a rape and second degree battery charge for my attack. Being an obvious repeat offender, he decided to plea out about a month after the attack. Unfortunately, I wasn't included in the discussions of the plea agreement, which wasn't all that uncommon at the time. I learned afterward that he received 3-terms of 40-years as his sentence. Sadly enough, part of the plea agreement allowed those 3-terms to run concurrent, and dropping the second degree battery charge altogether. I never completely agreed with why he wasn't charged with attempted murder in my case, being that was clearly his intentions, but I was told by the prosecution, *"It would have taken away from the rape charge."* I was thankful that I wouldn't have to testify in front a bunch of strangers about the most humiliating thing to ever happen to me, but I had definite issues with him only getting 40 years for raping and mutilating my body.

It took a couple of weeks for my blood red eyes to fade to a yellow, and then finally clearing to white soon thereafter. By the time I had my 8-week check up with my gynecologist and the Ear, Nose and Throat specialist, I had learned that my body was healing wonderfully. With the exception of the puffiness around my neck that has never completely vanished. If only I were healing emotionally as well as I appeared to be physically. The daylight hours weren't so bad, but the nights were another story altogether. I never wanted to be alone, and I seemed to constantly search for distractions. By August, I was drinking nightly before bed in hopes of just passing out. I just didn't want to deal with anymore flashbacks and I thought maybe I could just drown them out for a while. They were so real at times that I could feel that same intense fear, that dire need to get away. I got so tired of seeing that green hat coming after me night after night. By Labor Day, I was also smoking marijuana, because the alcohol alone wasn't helping me block out enough. And when I got to the point to where I wanted to avoid sleep altogether, I actually tried cocaine to help fight that. Crawling to bed every night in a drunken, stoned stupor wasn't exactly a healthy way to cope, but I had absolutely no other ideas as to how to deal with the chaos in my own mind. My mother had enough trouble trying to figure out her own issues, she certainly didn't know how to help me with mine. She just felt sorry for me. And dad basically tried to avoid serious conversations with me due to his own uncertainties about how to deal with the situation. I still hadn't seen or heard from the lady from the rape crisis center since that morning I was found. I really began to resent her statement that I wouldn't be alone. I was more alone now than ever, even though I had people around me most of the time. At one point I wondered if maybe she believed that I didn't need any help. And I wasn't ready to ask some other stranger for help just yet either.

Sadly enough, I continued to follow that path of self destruction for a while before waking one day, many months later, and thinking that there has got to be a better way. No matter how much I drank or smoked, it wasn't really helping. The self-medicating was only suppressing the problem for a little while, and it was always right there in my face once I sobered. By this time I had lost all of my ambition, most of my self-esteem, and even my faith. I blamed God for a very long time for allowing something like that to even happen to me, when I truly considered myself to be a decent person. The extent of prayer, for me, had become questioning. I just couldn't understand how He could allow such bad things happen to good people, and how even good things could happen to the bad. It hadn't yet dawned on me that it could have been God who kept me alive in those woods over night, or Him who made sure I felt no pain when I finally woke, or Him who sent the rescuing car along to help me escape that morning. Those were just a few of the things that I learned once I finally did turn to a stranger for help.

One day I heard a public service announcement on the radio for the local rape crisis center hotline, and called it. I can honestly say that that was a major turning point for me. I met an extremely inspiring woman who showed me the true meaning of unconditional support and tenacity. That was precisely what I needed most at that point in my life. The woman that I spoke with was Joye Cook, and she had just recently taken over the management of the local Rape Crisis Center. Apparently, the lady I remembered seeing in the trauma unit the morning I was rescued didn't tell anyone of me, or my case, before she left the Center. I guess you could say that I sort of fell through the cracks. I was so thankful that this new person I was speaking with seemed to show less pity, and more out right encouragement. The last thing I wanted, or needed for that matter, was for someone else to feel sorry for me. And thankfully she became a pillar of strength for me. She helped me see that there is good in this world, just as there is evil. She also gently pointed out that I had buried all of my emotions and fears deep within, rather than actually dealing with them. This one person took so much time from her own life in order to help me learn healthier ways of coping, as well as refreshing the strength of my faith. In the beginning, I honestly thought people were just being ridiculous when they said that talking about it helps you heal. It's awfully difficult to understand how reliving the past can help you move forward, but they were right. Before long, I was learning to control my fears, rather than letting them control me. I couldn't stand the fact that this one sadistic man could have so much control over me, as well as my life. The fear that I was harboring was his source of power. I had let that fear consume me to the point that, on one occasion, I found myself on the ground hyperventilating upon sight of a neon green baseball cap. So as my first big act of reclaiming control over my life, I went out and bought one of those bright green caps. Even though the sight of it made me sick to my stomach, as soon as I got home, I hung it in the living room. When I would get used to seeing it in one part of the house, I would move it into another. I continued this routine until the time came that I could look at it without any reaction other than anger, and then I finally threw it away. I know that isn't exactly a method that will work for everyone, but it was what worked for me. Just one of my new coping strategies was to face my fears head on.

As time went on, I saw that I was actually living in the shadow of that attack. In small towns, people talk… a lot! I couldn't hide from the fact that I was suddenly known as "the girl raped on Gravel Pit Road". No one wants to be known for something like that. So when I heard that there was a job opening at a local radio station, and that they usually preferred female personalities to create alternate characters for themselves, I jumped all over that opportunity. I finally felt some ambitious fire within me once again. The fact that I could give myself a whole new identity appealed to me immensely. I started out as receptionist in the front office. Then I began voicing commercials for them, and then a few months later they made me an on-air personality. After talking to a couple of other radio personalities, I learned that this was a business where you basically had to move around in order to move up the ladder. That was just one more alluring aspect to this career in my opinion. People didn't know the name I used, but so many always recognized my voice or my laugh. I knew then that no matter what I did, I would always be "that poor girl…" as long as I remained in the area I grew up in. There were so many reminders everywhere that I realized that it would be more difficult to learn how to heal if I couldn't reinvent myself in some way. So I decided to load what I could fit into my car and move to a neighboring state where my father lived. Thanks to the recommendations from the radio station where I previously worked, I had no problem getting a job at another station in this new state. Before long, I realized that I had made so many changes that I began to feel safer. I had a new name, lived in a new state, had a wonderful new career that I thoroughly enjoyed, and I felt that I could finally bury certain burdens of my past.

By the year 2000, I was living a rather productive life in southern Mississippi. I was blessed enough to have a family of my own; a good job at a local radio station, and no one knew anything about my past unless I told them myself. Early that year I began to experience some mild pelvic pain, but didn't think much of it at the time. At least until the pain seemed to get worse. It wasn't like menstrual cramps, but it was in the same general area. After a visit to my OB/GYN, he decided that he would have to do a Diagnostic Laparoscopy, a common exploratory surgery, to look inside of my abdominal cavity to see why I was having those increasing pains. What he found was that I had what is called adhesions throughout my rectal and vaginal cavities. After I described exactly what had happened to me 9 years earlier, it was explained to me that my body was essentially still trying to heal itself. I had so much internal scar tissue that, even after all those years, it was actually bonding together in a healing manner. I remember thinking, *"Great! I'm still being haunted by that incident."* This is about when the nightmares started coming back sporadically. They became even more frequent the following year when I received a notice in the mail form the Arkansas Department of Correction. My attacker's first parole hearing was right around the corner! By this time fear had reared its ugly head again, and I was suddenly dreaming of that sadistic rapist stalking my home, and peeking around bushes at my children. Once I started having these anxiety and panic attacks, I went to my doctor for help. I felt like I was losing control all over again. My doctor had given me Xanax to help me with the anxiety. For the next few years, I attended annual Victim Input Meetings with the Post Prison Transfer Board to protest my attacker's parole. These hearings were extremely difficult to endure. In order for these people to truly understand what kind of danger this man is to society, I had to open up old wounds. Thankfully, I wasn't ever alone during these hearings. I had the personal support of not only Joye Cook, but also the lead investigator from the Sheriffs Office, Greg Bolin. Without fail, they've always attended these meetings with me. That alone made it easier seeing the blown-up 8x10 photos of my battered face being passed around, in addition to hearing the details, yet again, of the extent of damage he inflicted not only upon me, but the torture he inflicted upon his prior victim as well. As a united force, we had to help the parole board see that this guy is a repeat offender. He's indisputably someone who will continue to get worse with each attack, and who obviously felt no remorse for his actions, only disappointment that he was caught.

For the first couple of years, I wasn't even able to attend these Victim Input Meetings without the aid of either Xanax or Valium. Then one year it dawned on me that I went from depending on illegal crutches to legal ones in order to help me cope. I then made it my mission to be able to attend these meetings completely drug free, so to speak. In early 2003, I was invited to a Christian retreat camp for a weekend with some friends from my church. One friend specifically, Cyndi Thornton, I had met a year earlier. She became a new source of liveliness and valor. We quickly discovered that we had both survived similar tragedies in our lives, and that we had so much in common that we couldn't help but become lifelong, devoted friends. She assured me that this retreat would be an experience like no other. I had never heard of 'Cursillo' before, but I was told that everyone who attends leaves with a new sense of purpose. Needless to say, that sincerely interested me. Now I don't want to ruin the surprise, or the experience, for anyone else that may go in the future, but this retreat became yet another turning point in my healing process, and I feel obliged to share. Upon arrival, I discovered that my friend Cyndi was there too, and would stay for the duration of the retreat as a member of the staff. The camp leaders immediately held a group prayer asking for God to help each of us understand what purpose we are there for. We we're all divided to cabins in groups, with no one knowing the others in the group. Once I was shown to my cabin, I was introduced to my weekend roommates. We all began to converse while we unpacked and got settled in. During this chat, not very long after arriving, one roommate began telling us about someone she knew who was recently found raped and beaten to death at just 17 years of age. The similarities were tremendously frightening to me. Through a sudden rush of tears that flooded my face, I felt as though this was God's way of explaining why I was there. That it was finally time for me to deal with those remaining buried emotions that I had been harboring for so very long. I also noticed that there was one specific word that kept popping up time and again over the weekend... Persevere. I hadn't ever given that word much thought, until then. To persevere, you must carry on, continue, and persist. That word, and its meaning, really seemed to stick in my mind. Later during that weekend, we were asked to kneel at the foot of a wooden cross that was propped up in the sanctuary and leave our heaviest burdens there for God to handle. I remember going down on my knees, begging Him to take away all of the fear, anxiety, reservations, and confusion. I remember telling myself that I'll not take these burdens back, that they were no longer mine. I had carried them long enough, and His shoulders were certainly stronger than mine. I can honestly say that once I stood I felt a true sense of comfort, of peace. To this day I avow that Cursillo #109 was when I finally learned how to persevere. The very next parole protest meeting that I attended, I was incredibly proud to declare that I was completely free of any prescribed assistance. Even my panic attacks were finally under control.

After many years of attending the annual meetings to protest the parole of my attacker, the parole board finally decided that they would refuse any further hearings until he completed the sex offenders program provided through the

Department of Corrections. I was very appreciative for that decision, being that he wasn't showing any interest in that program whatsoever. This was about when I decided that it would be incredibly beneficial for me to better educate myself on people like him, and many of the circumstances that encourage sexual predators. I realized the best way to reduce the occurrence of rape is to inform potential victims of preventative measures and escape techniques. I learned that they're almost always opportunists. Similar to animal predators that stalks their prey. They watch others, plan their attack, and then wait for the opportunity. The victim depends on who was in the wrong place at the wrong time. For many people, someone having the element of surprise over you can be temporarily disabling, exactly as it was for me after receiving that very first punch to my face. The shock of what was happening caused me to momentarily freeze while my inebriated mind tried to process what was going on. This awareness helped me decide that I should take some self defense classes so that I could feel more confident in protecting myself. Taking those classes was unquestionably one of the most empowering things I had done for myself! I only wished that I had taken them sooner. Nothing can make a woman feel more competent than being able to put a 300 pound man to the floor in only a few swift moves. This was a tremendous boost to my self confidence, and one that I would certainly recommend to other survivors.

Whenever I traveled back to Arkansas to attend the protest parole meetings, Joye Cook and I would always have lunch afterward, before parting ways to head back home. During one of these luncheons, she asked me what I thought about talking to others about my story. Even after her explanation that it could possibly help other people, I couldn't help but feel a little apprehension over the thought of standing in front of a bunch of strangers and talking about the most mortifying experience to ever occur in my life. I agreed to think it over as optimistically as possible. After returning to my home in central Mississippi later that day, I talked it over with my best friend Cyndi. She went on to explain I could possibly help other women learn how not to appear as an easy target through a predators eyes. She also felt that I could inspire other victims to learn ways to empower themselves. The more I thought about it, the more I rationalized that this could be a way of producing something positive out of such a traumatic experience.

I made the decision to try out my public speaking skills first on those I felt more comfortable around. My very first telling of my experience was in front of my church congregation. I was very appreciative of that simply because I already knew most of the people there, and I felt I was in a safe and comfortable environment. I felt so encouraged by the immediate support I received, that I arranged my next speaking engagement to be with the local police department. Being that the chief there understood my concerns, as well as my need to share such an awful experience, he encouraged me to help his officers better understand what all is going on in the minds of victims of sexual assault. I actually felt more comfortable speaking in front of these officers than I originally thought I would. Within a year's time, I had attended a training seminar on working with child victims and witnesses, as well as several training courses from the National Organization for Victims Assistance (NOVA). All the while I was speaking publicly about sexual assault awareness in front of public and civic organizations, other church congregations, and even other police departments to help those officers better understand the effects of sexual violence. At first, it was rather surprising to hear that there had never been a survivor to stand in front of these officers to offer answers to questions that they might have, at least until I really began to think about it. Then I rationalized that there couldn't be very many survivors who felt comfortable enough to even consider doing that, so then I must at least try. All emergency responders should be aware of all the different ways that a victim could be further victimized by the responder making the wrong comment, causing the victim to clam up, thus failing in building a good rapport. They could even damage their investigative process, or hinder the healing progression for the victim, by simply not understanding the victim's reaction to such an experience. One thing that I always made sure that everyone understood was that you can never blame a person's criminal actions on the clothing worn by the victims. If your mother, sister or wife were on a beach wearing a bikini, would she really *deserve* to be raped? Would your daughter deserve to be sexually assaulted simply because a guy thought she looked irresistible in her cheer-leading uniform? Sounds rather ridiculous, doesn't it? I have never believed that any person could deserve such a tormenting occurrence. Blaming the victim only serves to sanction rape as a justifiable form of criminal behavior. There may be a few who have a hard time understanding that their actions or words could essentially re-victimize a victim of sexual violence. I've always suggested that if they weren't quite sure of what to say, then it's better to just say nothing at all. Sensitivity training isn't necessarily needed for first responders, but some common sense is definitely required. When a person makes a victim feel as though they asked for what happened, they're actually causing the victim to withdraw or shut down, thus breaking any chance of forming a basic trust so that the victim will open up more comfortably. The first responders can have a huge impact on how the victim heals and how much information the victim gives to law enforcement for future prosecution. Cooperation of all parties involved certainly makes this entire process much more tolerable.

Eventually, I shared a condensed version of my story through the radio station where I worked during Sexual Assault Awareness Month, though modified a little for family friendly listening. I was absolutely astonished by the amount of responses that were received. Within hours I was getting phone calls, e-mails and later even letters from other victims and survivors of sexual violence. It was the amount of bad experiences with a rape crisis center, law enforcement officer or overbearing family member that made me consider that there had to be a better way of informing more people on how to better understand everything that consumes victims of sexual violence, in addition to how their behaviors can effect their acceptance to move forward. It was a little humbling to hear other people say that after hearing about my incident and seeing how well I was getting along, gave them inspiration to learn how to better persist themselves. I had absolutely no idea that sharing this experience with others could be so inspiring. That indeed helped me believe that one person can truly make a difference. So I decided that after an 11 year career in the broadcast industry, I wanted to work exclusively with the awareness of sexual violence, and how to better protect society from its predators. I do still enjoy voicing commercials from time to time, especially for those organizations that continue to offer hope to victims of sexual violence.

A few years ago I learned that my attacker had convinced a young lady from a religious mission group that he was set-up by the state, that he was completely innocent. This poor girl then agreed to marry him during his incarceration. I felt such confusion as to how someone could possibly not see him for what he truly is. My heart does go out to her, being that she has no idea what she's in for once he's released. I fear that her naivety will be a grave error on her part; but one that I certainly hope she survives.

I have always been thankful for my years and experiences in broadcasting. It helped me find my voice, so to speak. It also helped me get over the intimidation of being able to stand in front of a group of strangers without my legs trembling until I collapsed. I'm far more comfortable now with speaking out when I find something unfair, when I would once remain silent to simply avoid drawing too much attention to myself. I suppose it also helped me change my overall perspective on life, and how I want to live it.

The more informed a person is, the less likely they will fall victim so easily. When I was younger, I remember hearing a Saturday morning cartoon telling us that "knowledge is power", and that is especially true nowadays. Sexual predators are everywhere. They live just down the block, go to the local grocery store, and they're even members of the neighborhood gym. Every female, from adolescent to adult, should know at least a few self defense/get away techniques. Rape is simply about control and power. When you learn to move on without letting that event control every aspect of your life, then you essentially strip the attacker of that power over you.

To all, I hope you're always cautious and mindful of the potential dangers around you. To other victims and survivors of sexual violence, I hope you persevere!

Sexual Assault Awareness

It's imperative to understand that rape is not the same as having sex. Since the same body parts are involved in sexual assault as in love making, many people confuse it with intercourse. Rape is literally an expression of power and/or control in which a person uses a sexual act as a means to dominate, humiliate and/or degrade the victim. There are various forms of rape, including: Acquaintance Rape, Date Rape, Spousal Rape, Child Sexual Abuse, Incest, Drug Facilitated Sexual Assault, Male Sexual Assault, and many more variations of the offense which differs per state. Survivors of any form of sexual violence are forced to learn how to cope with emotional chaos, while some people around them feel that the victim should be able to simply shake it off like a bad mood.

Sexual assault is one of the most emotionally traumatic and least reported crimes in the United States, and occurs every 2 minutes (5). It breaks a persons sense of safety, trust, and sometimes distorts the way the victim feels about intercourse in the future. Physical harm is only one aspect of sexual assault. Victims feel their view of the world as being a 'safe place' is shattered. Not to mention the feeling of losing control over their own lives and emotions. These things do take time to overcome, and each person will recover at a different rate of speed.

There's a very interesting study described in an article called 'Assessing Sexual Aggression' by E.D. Kolivas & A.M. Gross. They explain a study that compared male and female perceptions of date rape. Sawyer et al. 1998 (10), "presented 474 college students with one of eight written dating scenarios all ending in sexual intercourse. The levels of sexual coercion and consent were varied across the eight scenarios. Participants were asked to identify whether the man in the scenario used sexual coercion, if the female gave sexual consent, if rape occurred, and were asked if the man in the scenarios should be criminally charged or punished for the offense. Men evidenced greater difficulty than women interpreting ambiguous responses to sexual advances and were more likely to interpret a lack of verbal response as consent to sexual intercourse. Female respondents were better able than men to identify when consent was given and if coercive strategies were used in the ambiguous sexual encounter. Thus, it appears that ambiguous situations represent greater interpretive challenges to men than women (1)." Maybe that's an indication that men need to be taught sexual assault awareness even more so than women. This is something that should begin as young as adolescents, for males and females alike.

Research does suggest that men and women differ in how they interpret sexual involvement and their willingness to engage in sexual intercourse. This gender communication difference has been referred to as the "Miscommunication Hypothesis" (1). Sexual deviates intentionally count on those misinterpretations, and most are masters in the art of manipulation.

According to Rape, Abuse and Incest National Network (RAINN), 1-in-6 women, and 1-in-33 men, will be sexually assaulted in their lifetime. One of the most common misconceptions about sexual violence is that it only happens to young, pretty girls. In reality, these victims belong to both sexes, all races and ethnic groups, economic backgrounds, and even all ages. Sexual violence is something that knows no discrimination.

It is crucial for everyone to know their surroundings, at all times. This includes the street where you live, the encompassing neighborhoods, as well as the potential dangers around your child's school and other places they frequent. It only seems logical to educate yourself as to the type of people that live and work near places that you and your family enjoy. There are many websites out there today that can help inform you as to the dangers in your own backyard, so to speak. Some of these services allow you to see where registered sexual offenders live and work anywhere around you, and some can even notify you when a registered sex offender moves within 5-10 miles of a given address that you care about. A few will allow you to track offenders and send you notifications if the specified offender has a change in their living status. This is helpful knowledge to have when trying to become aware of the known offenders that could live or work near places that your family frequents. The more you know, the better you're able to prepare and protect. I do want to stress that there is a fine line between using this information to protect your family, and using these types of resources to stalk or harass someone. These are very helpful services that are intended to inform the public of the potential dangers in a certain community.

Convictions are most likely to occur in cases that fit the stereotypical rape, and are less likely when the woman knows her assailant; especially if they dated or had prior sexual contact. This bias is so strong on many levels of the legal system that some rape crisis counselors will go as far as to advise victims of acquaintance rape, with little or no evidence, to think very carefully before becoming involved in criminal proceedings. In cases where there's no solid evidence, the chances of successful prosecution are quite slim, and sometimes the victim doesn't see the benefits of going through the process if they know there's likely no positive outcome.

I've read some reports that stated that the typical sexual predator will assault 110-120 times before being caught. Now multiply that estimate by the fact that there are approximately 559,000 registered sex offenders in the United States. Now can you get an idea of the number of victims, and the amount of psychological trauma, each offender created. Can you even begin to imagine the number of sex offenders that aren't registered, simply making roots where ever they like? It also seems that about 45% of rapists released from prison are re-arrested within 3-5 years of their release for another crime. If you're like me, then you're thinking that something has got to change. One way to combat that problem is to better inform and empower those who are potential victims... which are just about anyone and everyone. It appears that we're simply recycling these sexual predators in and out of society, even after so many years of failed attempts at rehabilitating such behaviors and thought patterns. Now I know that there are a few people who will argue that some sexual offenders can indeed be rehabilitated, and possibly lead perfectly normal lives without ever offending again. My point is that even with all the attempts at rehabilitating sexual predators, there are far too many who re-offend within just a few years of such treatment. This alone makes most people feel that the majority can never be rehabilitated, but only closely monitored. I strongly favor the idea that all registered sexual offenders should wear ankle monitors. Not only are they less expensive to maintain, but they can also provide the offenders location if there is a sexual offense in the area. That doesn't exactly help track those offenders who haven't been convicted, but it would certainly help track those who fail to register or try removing the monitors themselves.

Tips for Prevention

The best method to protecting yourself is through prevention. By not putting yourself into defenseless positions, you've already greatly reduced your chances of being victimized. Below are many more tips that can help prevent your placement in a vulnerable situation.

- Always be alert to your surroundings.

- Walk with confidence and trust your gut instincts.

- Always have your keys ready before you reach your car.

- Avoid distractions while walking; such as texting, digging in your purse or bag for your keys, etc.

- Don't listen to iPods and Walkmans while out walking or running. You need to be aware of all of the sounds around you as well.

- Never leave a social event with someone you've just met.

- Be smart when it comes to drugs and alcohol. These will certainly cloud your judgment and delay your reactions.

- Be extra careful at social events where the use of alcohol or drugs are commonly shared or encouraged.

These places are very appealing to those who are looking to slip a little something into your drink.

- Avoid walking anywhere alone, especially at night. You should also avoid walking away with people that you hardly know.

- If you're at a bar or club, never leave your drink unattended.

- If possible, always carry a cell phone and some means of defensive protection.

- If your car breaks down, turn on your emergency flashers, lock your doors, stay in your car and call for help.

- At home, never invite a stranger inside, and don't trust the door chain, they're not dependable!

- Always check the identification of any sales people that come to your home and call their office for confirmation. It's a good idea to have another adult with you when service people come to your house, if you can arrange that.

- Have a peep hole installed in your door and a well lit entrance-way.

- Be sure to lock your windows and doors, especially at night.

- Never travel alone, if it can be helped. It's better to develop a buddy system with a friend so that neither of you will be alone at any time. If you must travel alone, then make sure you give someone else your travel plans so that they are able to relay that information should you not contact them after a certain amount of time.

- When outdoors, stay within range of people, where someone can always see and hear you.

- If asked directions or the time, remain at a safe distance, ready to react if necessary.

- If you're alone in an elevator and someone that makes you uncomfortable steps in, step out immediately.

- Never give all your keys to a parking attendant. Remove the key the attendant needs, and then keep the rest with you.

- Always have someone escort you to your car after dark.

- If you jog or walk daily, vary your route and routines. Predators prefer predictability.

- Try to stay on sidewalks when able, avoiding bushes, fences and doorways.

- Always remain in well lit areas at night, and it's not a bad idea to carry a flashlight with you.

- Know your way around buildings that you frequently visit.

- If you feel you're being followed while driving, pull into a public place or drive directly to the nearest police station.

- Always make sure that you have enough gas to get to your destination.

- If you use public transportation, always be alert to your surroundings, as well as those who exit with you.

- Be cautious when entering public restrooms that are in the back of buildings or secluded.

- Never pick up strangers or hitchhikers, ever!

"People don't ever seem to realize that doing what's right is no guarantee against misfortune."

~William McFee

In Case Of Attack...

Unfortunately, not all girls are being taught how to handle situations like this before they occur; which is especially scary when you remember the fact that 1 in 6 women will experience sexual violence at some point in their lives. There's an amazing non-profit organization, formed by 16 year old Dallas Jessup, which is making a monumental impact on the lives of young girls everywhere. "Just Yell Fire", based in Portland, Oregon, has the sole mission of keeping teenage girls safe from assault, abduction, and even death by teaching them that they have the right to fight back, in addition to giving them the skills to put a stop to date rape and putting predators out of business. Though targeted towards younger girls, I strongly advise every female to learn these techniques! There is an excellent film available on www.justyellfire.com that teaches you easy, yet extremely effective, ways to get-away from an attacker.

If you're under attack:

When it comes to handling an attacker, everything depends on the situation, your emotional and physical state, and the offender's personality. Remember, surviving is the ultimate goal! When methods of prevention fail, and you're approached by a rapist, it's very important that you remain calm. Panic can cause you to freeze up, and you need to focus now more than ever.

- If someone is coming into your personal space, hold your hands out in front of you and yell 'STOP' or 'STAY BACK'.

- Stall for time while accessing your options and surroundings. You must look for ways to escape. If the attacker has a weapon, you may have no choice but to submit. Do whatever it takes to survive!

- Yell "FIRE" rather than "HELP", or "RAPE".

- If you decide to fight back, you must be determined, persistent and effective in your actions. If you see an opportunity, act on it immediately!

If you've already been attacked:

- Get to a safe place immediately!

- Contact a friend, relative, neighbor, etc. There are many people available to give you the emotional support that you'll need. Many law enforcement agencies even have a Victim Assistance Coordinator that can assist you through much, if not most, of the processes to follow.

- Seek medical attention immediately. DO NOT shower or clean up first. It's very important to get examined and treated for possible venereal diseases or pregnancy. You may also have internal injuries you're not aware of.

- You can report the attack to the police, whether

or not you plan to file charges. Rarely do rapists attack only one person; they may get away with it and continue to rape. At least then the authorities would know of the attack, and the perpetrator, even if you didn't press charges.

- DO NOT change or destroy your clothes. If you plan to press charges, then your clothing is evidence. It is a good idea to have someone bring you a change of clothes that you can wear home once you're released from the examination. (Even if you don't think you want to press charges, initially, you may change your mind and you'll need all of the evidence.)

- Contact your local rape crisis center or the National Sexual Assault Hotline. You've just been through an extremely traumatic ordeal, and your greatest benefit would be to immediately learn healthy methods of coping and healing.

- Self-medication is never a healthy way to cope with such a traumatic experience. Sometimes medication is necessary, but should always be discussed with, and prescribed by, your doctor.

- Start keeping a journal of sorts, where you can write down your memories and thoughts throughout the healing process. A journal is also helpful during prosecution phase.

Rape Crisis Centers and Victim Advocates

I spent close to a year trying to mentally cope with the emotional effects of rape on my own. I found many ways to smother the fear and confusion for a short time, but nothing that gave me any long term results. I could have reduced that time dramatically if only I had reached out sooner. Generally, survivors who get counseling recover from an attack quicker, and with fewer lasting effects, than survivors who get no help at all. No one can force you to call a crisis center hotline, but they are there to help guide you to an understanding of how the system works, and how prosecution would work for you. There are a wide range of services available that will help you, if you only give them the opportunity. Frequently, rape crisis centers can assist you in identifying your specific needs, and then they can either provide you with the appropriate resources or refer you to other local resources for any of the following services:

- Individual counseling

- Group counseling/support groups

- Legal/criminal justice system advocacy

- Victim assistance advocacy

- Community education

- Professional education

- Casework/practical assistance

- Emergency shelter

- Hospital Accompaniment

There are even some advocates who will help the victim prepare and plan for court appearances, primarily to counter comments that the defense might make regarding revealing clothing and such. This is a major change in the role of advocates over the last 20 years or so. After suffering many years of the defense attacking the victim over their personal appearance at court proceedings, many advocates decided that by providing some guidance in courtroom attire they could help alleviate that added stress.

You may not even realize that many of the people that work with these types of agencies have either been affected by sexual violence in their own lives or in the life of someone they care about. Many more of them have some of the most compassionate hearts that you'll find anywhere. They receive calls from victims hours, weeks, or even years after the attack. These advocates are trained to openly listen to your needs, and then determine what services would better help you. There's no need to either hide your feelings from them, or feel embarrassed in any way. You will not be judged or criticized by true advocates. Not to mention that these centers are staffed with trained individuals who focus solely on helping victims learn how to become survivors. They understand that sometimes extreme levels of embarrassment can cause you to withhold certain details at first, but I encourage you to trust them. Since the conversations between the victim and advocate/counselor are privileged, you don't have to worry about them telling anyone else anything you share. They can truly help get you on the path to healing much faster.

You may not be able to change what happened to you, but you can seek justice in order to prevent it from happening to someone else. You can also discover methods to exercise power and control over your life, while allowing yourself time to properly heal emotionally. Every victim deserves to learn how to live free of fear. This can be more challenging for some victims than others. As you may well imagine, reporting rates are considerably lower in many rural communities, primarily due to the lack of privacy in small towns. These victims also seek help far less than victims who live in larger cities. Not so long ago, there were no other options for the victims who lived in such small areas, and it can feel like everyone knows what happened to you. Today we have quite a few national networks offering each and every victim the much needed guidance and support, despite where they live. If you don't feel comfortable going to your local rape crisis center, for whatever reason, I would at least ask that you consider turning to a confidential national organization help-line, like the National Sexual Assault Hotline, operated by RAINN. (1-800-656-HOPE) You're still able to get that much needed assistance, while holding on to your sense of privacy. Often, they can refer you to someone in your area that can help guide you through these difficulties while understanding and respecting your sense of privacy. In the Helpful Resources section in the back of this book there are a few other national organizations offering free, confidential support to any victim wishing to learn how to become a survivor.

"Perseverance is not a long race; it is many short races, one after another."

~ Walter Elliott

Reporting to the Police

Whether or not to report your attack is your decision alone. There is much to take into consideration when deciding whether or not to report or press charges. There are multiple factors that can make a victim feel as though they're suffering re-victimization through the legal processes. It's as loathsome having evidence collected from your person as is discussing embarrassing details with complete strangers, and risking a breach of confidentiality by telling other people what happened feeds the apprehension of being disbelieved and/or ridiculed by other people. Not to mention the torment of having to endure a cross-examination by some aggressive defense attorney whose sole mission is to prove that his/her client is innocent. If there is little or no evidence, then this process can be even more complicated. Thankfully, in many areas, it's now possible to report your attack without pressing charges. This reporting procedure can be a long, grueling process that can truly test a person's emotional and physical endurance. If you are planning to report the attack, it's a good idea to start writing down everything you remember about it. Write down the attackers description, describe the attack itself, things the attacker may have said, even certain smells you noticed can be relevant. Keeping a journal is often suggested to not only give you a clear account that details the attack itself, but also to help you keep track of your progression throughout the healing process. The more time passes, the fuzzier some details will get. Writing it down will prove helpful in recalling details should the victim be required to testify, but it also gives the survivor an active role in the investigative and prosecution processes. This can allow for a feeling of empowerment and an element of control in a situation where control had previously been taken away.

When it's time to tell the police what happened, try to stay focused on describing the attack, step-by-step. It's too easy to get sidetracked onto another topic when also dealing with psychological trauma. Just try to stay focused on describing exactly what happened. It's also important to speak clearly so that the investigators can more easily follow your descriptions. If you're unsure about a question, it's okay to ask them to return to that question later. You must understand that when reporting the attack, you will have to answer some very difficult and uncomfortable questions. You'll have to help investigators understand every aspect of the attack; from what was done, to how and where it was done. Some questions could even make an investigator feel crude or discourteous, but they understand the importance. There's also no need for you to have to endure this process unassisted. If you don't already have someone that you want to be with you during this procedure, then there are other options. You may either use the crisis counselor provided through many law enforcement agencies, or you can request an advocate through the rape crisis center. Most officers are more than willing to help with this accommodation, understanding that when the victim feels comfortable they are more likely to cooperate throughout the investigative process. Most officers also know that when the victim is distressed and embarrassed, then they could have a difficult time getting accurate information detailing the attack. That's the main reason that most victim advocates would prefer to be able to talk with the victim for a short time before they make their official statement for the record. In those cases, the entire interview will usually flow much smoother, and typically is less time consuming. Everyone involved at this stage knows that the victim may feel foolish, hurt, ashamed, vulnerable, frightened, and most likely even questioning their judgment. Understand that this may be a difficult stage to get through, and it could be very time consuming, but some survivors have stated that they found strength and encouragement by remembering that this has to be done in order to help prevent the attacker from doing this to someone else.

When you consider that about 84 percent of sexual assaults go unreported (4), you can just imagine the amount of unresolved trauma. The assailants aren't held accountable for their crimes, and law enforcement officials are left uninformed about the extent of sexual violence in their communities. In these cases the offender simply continues to wreak havoc, leaving behind a wake of emotional turmoil. According to the FBI, only 16 percent of victims of sexual violence report the crime to law enforcement (4). Victims of a rape by a stranger are more likely to report the crime than victims who are raped by people they know.

Major Changes in Reporting

I recently read a feature article on the FBI's website about the developments over the past decade of the option victims have in reporting sexual violence. If anonymous reporting is implemented in more jurisdictions, then there could be a double benefit.

The first paragraph read... "Blind reporting can give victims of sexual violence, and other sensitive crimes, a safe haven to file a report at the same time that it removes that refuge from their assailants. For the victim, the benefit of such a system lies in having time to build trust with the law enforcement officer and to consider all of the implications of participating in reporting, investigating, or prosecuting the case *before* making a decision whether to proceed. For the law enforcement agency, this type of reporting can help gain intelligence about the local incidence and perpetration of all sexual violence in the community, as well as build trust and credibility with populations vulnerable to assault.(4)"

It's amazing to me that such a natural concept could be so ground breaking. There are great populations of victims who never report their attacks to anyone for various different reasons. I am certain that if the concept of Blind Reporting is embraced and supported across the nation, then this could not only benefit the victims' sense of privacy, but also assist the law enforcement officials in gathering information related to sexually violent crimes.

My thoughts suddenly took me back to our countries early settlers, populating a vast new land. I remembered reading stories of women rejecting unwanted advances, only to be forced into a deplorable marriage after being raped. Could you even imagine being forced to make such a bond with your rapist? Then again, if you think back to what we know about the 13th century, certain religions were trying to debate whether or not women possessed souls as men did. To think the people of that time actually saw this consideration as rational reasoning. At least we've moved well past the period when rape was considered a justifiable means of claiming a woman. But to help us go even further, I encourage you to visit the FBI website in order to learn the basic steps in helping to establish a Restricted Reporting System in your area.

Evidence Collection

The medical-forensic examination is most certainly humiliating, and is often seen as a continuation of the traumatic experience. This process is physically uncomfortable and may even feel emotionally demeaning, but if you plan to press charges then this is a crucial step in that process. The National Center for Victims of Crime explains that "preserving the DNA evidence can be key to identifying the perpetrator in a sexual assault case, especially those in which the offender is a stranger. DNA evidence is an integral part of an investigation that can build a strong case to show that a sexual assault occurred and to show that the defendant is the source of biological material left on the victim's body (6)."

Victims should make every effort to save anything that might contain the perpetrator's DNA, therefore a victim should not:

- Bathe or shower

- Use the restroom

- Change clothes

- Comb or brush hair

- Clean up the crime scene

- Move anything the offender may have touched

Even if the victim has not yet decided to report the crime, receiving a forensic medical exam, and keeping the evidence safe from damage, will improve the chances that the police can access and test the stored evidence at a later date, as long as the statute of limitations hasn't ran its course.

These types of exams are generally performed at a hospital or other healthcare facility, by a sexual assault nurse examiner (SANE), sexual assault forensic examiner (SAFE) or another medical professional. This exam is complex and on average, takes a few hours. While this may seem lengthy, medical and forensic exams are comprehensive because the victim deserves and needs special attention to ensure that they are medically safe and protected. The evidence will be collected with what is commonly called a Rape Kit. RAINN explains "the Rape Kit is generally a large envelope or cardboard box, which safely stores evidence collected from your body and/or clothing." While the contents of a sexual assault forensic exam may vary by state and jurisdiction, it may include items, such as:

- Instructions
- Bags and sheets for evidence collection
- Swabs
- Comb
- Envelopes for hair and fibers
- Blood collection devices

- Documentation forms

Under the *Violence Against Women and Department of Justice Reauthorization Act of 2005*, states may not "require a victim of sexual assault to participate in the criminal justice system or cooperate with law enforcement in order to be provided with a forensic medical exam, reimbursement for charges incurred on account of such an exam, or both." Under this law, a state must ensure that victims have access to an exam free of charge or with a full reimbursement, even if the victim decides not to cooperate with law enforcement investigators. Previously, states were required to ensure access to exams free of charge, but could put conditions on the exam, such as cooperating with law enforcement officials (5). Everyone should be examined following a sexual assault, whether the victim decides to press charges or not. At least this way, the evidence can be collected and saved while the victim makes his/her decision.

There are many reasons why victims of sexual violence would refuse to seek medical attention following an attack. If they knew their attacker, they may fear retribution for telling. Some may feel they can't afford the medical visit if they are uninsured. Many simply don't want the treatment to show up on their insurance or billing records. These are all logical concerns, but should be thoroughly discussed with a local advocate or counselor before making decisions. Many of these concerns can be remedied thanks to the efforts of advocates.

The Criminal Justice Process

Sexual Assault is, without a doubt, the hardest crime in which to get a conviction. The less evidence there is, the more difficult it is to get a successful prosecution. Following through the steps of the Criminal Justice System can be nerve wrecking, but it can also be a way of finding some form of resolution. There are various stages to this part of the process, which vary from state to state, and it can take anywhere from a month to a few years for it to come to a final conclusion. I would definitely advise you to choose a friend or two to provide you with the emotional support that you'll need. A friend or family member can be comforting, but there are times when no one is available, especially if the victim is new to an area. Some victims feel more embarrassed speaking so openly about the attack in front of family members. In those circumstances I would suggest calling in some local support that truly understands confidentiality and the process in which you're about to experience. Many prosecutors' offices and law enforcement agencies now have Victim/Witness programs that staff people to work closely with victims of sexual violence once they have decided to report and/or prosecute their attacker(s). These criminal justice system-based service providers can assist a victim in filing for state crime victim compensation funds; will file a restitution claim with the Court; will notify a victim of hearings, possible plea negotiations and court schedule changes; will accompany a survivor to various court proceedings; will explain the legal process and legal proceedings to the survivor; and will interact on the behalf of the victim's interests with the various attorneys, court personnel, and the survivor's employer or school. You can basically think of this person as a liaison between you and the criminal justice system.

During the actual court proceedings, the defense will try their best to make the police, and the victim, look incompetent. If they see that the victim looks uncomfortable, then they will feed on that. If the victim is to testify, then make certain that he/she is clear and confident in their statements. The victim will have to explicitly describe who put what where, when and how.

Many survivors have stated that choosing to follow through with prosecution contributed to a feeling of accomplishment and empowerment, mainly because they're attempting to protect themselves and others in the community from being victimized. Many victims also say that the actual attempt to put their attacker(s) in jail allows for a sense of closure, enabling them to put the assault behind them more readily.

Statute of Limitations

As explained on the RAINN website, Statutes of Limitations are laws that set the maximum amount of time that can pass after a crime is committed before legal action is taken (5). Statutes do vary by each state and by the type of offense. Once that time limit has expired, it's no longer possible to prosecute for that crime. Most states have statutes of limitations ranging from 5-10 years, but some have no set time limitation whatsoever. Additionally, there are a few states that allow for the prosecution of child sexual abuse for 20-30 years after the victim's 18th birthday. Availability of DNA evidence in sexual assault cases also has altered statutes of limitations. Many states extend, and others eliminate, the statute of limitations on specific sexual offenses if the identity of the perpetrator is proved by DNA evidence.

If you would like to know the Statute of Limitations of a sexual offense for your state, then I urge you to visit the RAINN website. You will find this information under the category of Public Policy Issues. Simply click on the state of interest to open a PDF file containing that information.

Also know that if a parent or guardian knows that their minor child has been sexually violated in any way, it's required by law to report that crime to the local authorities. It is considered negligent to refuse to report such a crime when a minor is involved.

"Every time you meet a situation, though you think at the time it is an impossibility and you go through the torture of the damned, once you have met it and lived through it, you find that forever after you are freer than you were before."

~Eleanor Roosevelt

A Healthy Healing Process

Many times during my healing process I wished that there were more ways for me to learn other methods that victims have used in order to get back control over their lives, specifically their emotions and fears. Most of the methods that you read in this book are either ones that I learned myself, or were shared by other survivors that I've known over the years.

There are many ways of dealing with the emotional whirlwind that one faces following an assault. Some victims seek the proper support afterward and learn positive ways to move towards healing. There are also some who try to bury their uncertainties by using self-medication as a means to momentarily relieve their emotional suffering. Self-medicating is not something that will produce a cure, since it only blankets the problem temporarily. Being that I tried avoidance and self-medicating as a means of coping first, my actual healing process was delayed. I could have saved myself many sleepless nights, and much confusion, had I called the crisis center hotline sooner. If a victim doesn't have a person with a sound mind to help them think through the chaos, then they are more likely to make unhealthy coping decisions. Not to mention the fact that the whole healing process is difficult enough without having to add in the problems that follow irrational choices in coping methods.

You should also understand that a victim cannot be forced through the healing process either, because they won't truly attempt to heal until they're absolutely ready. It's important to understand that there's no time limit on this healing phase, as each victim will recover at their own pace. Most of these victims are already trying to sort through such immense mental confusion that it's often difficult to know for certain what is reasonable and what is irrational. Having level-headed support during this time can be exactly what the victim needs in order to feel confident enough to commence healing.

There are quite a few methods to rationally help you manage those uncontrolled emotions. Find something that you enjoy, that allows you to concentrate and focus. When you feel you're losing control over your thoughts and emotions, engage in that activity. I've spoken to many victims who've found comfort or repose in Pilates, yoga, meditation, even energy medicine. I've also known a few who preferred arts and crafts as a distraction method. Whatever interests you and helps you redirect your focus will work. One victim started making friendship bracelets with embroidery string. Whenever she felt her mind begin to race, she'd grab the strings and start counting off knots in a set pattern. The repetitive motions were soothing to her, and once she felt back in control, then she'd put the bracelet aside until needed again. This helped her to learn better control over when she allowed herself to think about what happened to her. I discovered my love for reading as a means of distraction. Even now I indulge in my appreciation of nature and hiking, which provide many breathtaking views and sweet serenity for a little meditation time. I've found creating stained glass mosaic artwork is also quite therapeutic for me. I like creating my own designs and the challenge of making it look just right through each step of the process. Not only do you get a sense of satisfaction from what you accomplish, but the focus can also be a considerable distraction from unwanted emotions you may be feeling. If those types of activities don't spark your interest, then there are literally thousands of other things that you could do to get the same effects. If you love music, learn to play a new instrument. You may even find solace in drawing, painting, floral arrangements, sewing, reading, writing, you name it. I have even known a couple of survivors who decided to volunteer in local youth centers or animal rescue agencies and found they were better able to reconnect with their own emotions through helping those that were also in need. My point is, no matter the activity or hobby you chose, you can benefit from it as long as it's something that you truly enjoy doing. The one activity I've found to be universally beneficial to all victims is keeping a journal. This is where you write down memories, fears, goals, track your healing progress, etc. I felt as though writing in my journal helped me put my own thoughts and fears into better perspective. This may not sound very therapeutic at the moment, but it honestly does have great benefits if taken seriously.

One of the most brilliant choices you could make is joining a support group. Not only will you no longer feel alone in that struggle, but you'll also have the opportunity to give as much support as you receive. These meetings with other survivors prove to be a good source of finding new coping methods that have been beneficial to others. I do understand that there are some people who simply have no interest in sitting with a group of strangers to discuss such a distasteful common issue, but if you could manage to go to just a few of these meetings then you may meet another survivor, who has healed, that you click with. Becoming a support system for each other can be just has affective in healing. Just as my best friend Cyndi and I had done. We understood each other, could be open and honest about our fears, and we helped each other conquer them one at a time. It's amazing how you can pull such strength and courage from another person you feel close to. I was lucky enough to have Joye Cook earlier in my healing and Cyndi in my latter part. Between the both of them, I never felt as though I had no one I could talk to when struggling, or no one that could understand the difficulties involved. Both of them helped me feel as though I could ultimately overcome anything.

With the latest in modern technology, connecting with other victims or finding moral support has never been easier. There are many websites today that offer beneficial resources, as well as chat room for victims to connect. I've known many survivors who've structured internet support groups specifically for survivors of sexual violence. Be sure that you verify the authenticity of any group that you're interested in joining, in person and on the internet. A creditable one will give you basic information without requiring you to register, and should have someone of organizational status contact you should you request verbal or email reassurances. In the back of this book, under Helpful Resources, I've listed a few different organizations that I am rather familiar with, and know of their stability and credibility. Just remember that if you chose to use any public chat room, be cautious of the personal information that you release about yourself. These sites are vigilant in the protection of their users, but limiting the personal content is just an extra precaution to help protect you.

What to Expect from Victims

Sexual violence affects a person's body, emotions, thoughts, behavior and spirituality. Every survivor will react differently, depending on how they ordinarily cope with dilemmas in their life. There are no set reactions that each one follows, and each one will recover at a different speed. These reactions could vary from crying, laughing, joking or even refusing emotions altogether. Below is a list of some common effects of sexual violence.

- Nightmares and Flashbacks

- Anxiety or Shaking

- Mood swings / Shifts

- Loss of Control / Powerless

- Dissociation

- Easily Distressed

- Difficulty concentrating

- Fear

- Guilt / Shame

- Anger

- Aggressive fantasies

- Embarrassment

- Concern for Reputation / Image

- Emotional detachment

- Fight or Flight Urges

- Post Traumatic Stress Disorder (*P.T.S.D.*)

- Substance Abuse

- Sleep Disorders

- Eating Disorders

- Body Memories (Somatic Symptoms)

As described by RAINN, Body Memories are when the stress of the memories of the assault experienced by an individual take the form of physical problems that cannot be explained by usual means like medical examinations. These conditions are often called "psychosomatic symptoms" which does not mean that it is "in your head." Rather, it means that the symptoms are due to the connection between the mind and the body. Physical problems that can come of these somatic memories include headaches, migraines, stomach difficulties, light headed/dizziness, hot/cold flashes, grinding of teeth, sleep disorders, etc. These maladies can often be as frustrating for the survivor who is experiencing them as they are difficult to diagnose and cure, and may even add to the difficulty of recovery. With the appropriate guidance and counseling, they can learn to overcome the emotional trauma and even help ease many problematic symptoms (5).

Remember that it's not at all uncommon for a victim to experience more than one of these effects at a time, or for the degree to vary form one victim to another. You may also notice that the victim's story could change a little from one day to the next. Many times the victim will remember more details of the attack as time passes. This is quite normal, and is the main reason why many victim advocates would rather a victim speak to them prior to making their official recorded interview with the local police department. The most important step for a victim is to either find, or create, the right support system that will help them regain control over his/her own life. All victims need to feel empowered in order to find the courage to move towards healing.

There's a truly inspiring woman I know who created an online support system for victims of sexual and domestic violence. For some survivors, this site provides their primary source of strength and inspiration. Take A Stand Against Violence is a non-profit organization that provides a safe, online community to help support victims in becoming survivors. If you have survived some form of sexual violence, then you can benefit greatly from this online community. They also have a section on their website designated to help victims rise above the fear and uncertainty. If you know of someone who could benefit from this type of support, then make sure they visit www.tkastnd.org.

*"Fear is the most devastating of all human emotions.
Man has no trouble like the paralyzing effects of fear."*
                                                    ~Paul Parker

Other Obstacles Victims Face

There are many obstructions that a victim must overcome in order to move into a healthy healing process. The immediate effects are only part of the battle. The more time that passes, along with healthy coping strategies, the pain and confusion will eventually begin to fade. Sometimes the lines of healthy and unhealthy coping strategies can be confusing, to the victim as well as to loved ones.

I once spent some time with a teenage girl who had trouble sleeping on top of her bed following her attack. Her parents were so confused by this, being that the attack had not occurred in her room. They were worried that she wouldn't be able to move into a healing phase through this type of odd behavior. I first asked them if there was any form of personal injury involved, or likely to occur, with her decision, and they said there wasn't. Then I inquired if there would be any long term damage by letting her sleep under her bed for as long as she felt it necessary? They seemed to think about that question for a minute, and then said they didn't feel there would be. So I asked that they give her a little time to see just how long she feels that necessary. She continued to sleep under her bed for almost a month, before finally feeling safe enough to sleep atop. She is doing very well now, but told me that she felt too exposed and vulnerable being on top of her bed. She simply went through a period where felt as though she were more protected underneath. A victim can make some bizarre choices following an assault, so for obvious reasons they should not make drastically important decisions for a reasonable amount of time following. As long as the victim isn't causing any harm to themselves or anyone else, allow them to decide what makes them feel safe and in control. As their confidence builds and security grows, their strategies will evolve as well. However, if you truly see behavior that could be damaging, encourage the victim to confide in his/her counselor, therapist, or doctor in making sure that he/she is using the best coping methods for their situation.

In cases where the assailant is incarcerated, you should be aware that you are likely to experience a new wave of nightmares once your attacker is eligible for parole. This is also likely to occur during the trial phase. Remember that you always have a choice. You can either transform and renew, or you can retreat and forfeit to fear. This is a good time to reinvent yourself, and begin a new life. Being a part of a strong support group, or other support system that encourages positive reinforcement, can help you learn various ways to help transform yourself.

Another common issue that stems from sexual violence is confusion regarding intimate relations. So many victims develop an alternate opinion of intimacy following an attack, ranging from desensitizing themselves to it to completely avoiding intimacy altogether. I actually went through a phase of desensitizing myself to intimacy, telling myself that it meant very little or nothing at all. It was just an action that didn't involve emotions. It takes time to overcome, but it can be done with the proper guidance and support. By nature, we are social creatures, so it isn't normal to avoid other people or social situations anymore than it is to numb yourself to emotions. It's vital to find reasonable means of getting by, and professional guidance can suggest rational methods of coping with the distressing thoughts or feelings that will arise as time passes.

Spouses and Partners of Victims

The aftereffect of sexual violence has destroyed more relationships than you could ever begin to imagine. It puts a completely different strain on a partner than it does for any other family member, being that those are the ones we share a certain intimacy with. Sometimes the victim has trouble with the physical contact involved, and sometimes the partner of the victim isn't able to comprehend the emotional effects that follow such an attack. A great many victims develop mixed emotions about sexual relations, and their partners may even have trouble understanding this confusion. It's common for them to believe that they love and care for the victim, and that they're not the attacker... so there shouldn't be any confusion. In reality, the sexual act of rape causes a considerable amount of mental trauma. The mind may have flashbacks during intercourse due to a certain position or from finding some relevance in the sexual act itself. It's better not to dwell on how terrible the act was, and you certainly shouldn't suggest that he/she should have been more careful, EVER! That lays blame, and if you're going to place blame anywhere then put it in the one who committed the crime. Never on the victim, as this will cause further stress and confusion, thus delaying the progression of coming to terms with what happened so they can begin healing.

One of the best ways to help a victim is to be there, and be patient. Create alone time for talks, and then let them talk, so that they can better sort out their own confusion. You may find it difficult to openly listen when he/she needs to talk about their feelings, especially details of the attack itself. Be considerate of what your partner may be feeling and remain calm, without passing judgment. This is an important element in order to move towards the healing process and cannot be avoided, so try not to let your own emotions interfere. Remember, this isn't about you. Make sure you assure the victim that the attack was not his/her fault. It may also be confusing when the survivor continues to be affected for weeks, months, and even years down the road. There is no time limit, and they will all recover at their own pace. You may even feel guilty or responsible; believing that you should have some how prevented the assault. All of these feelings are understandable following an assault of someone you love. Please know that if feelings are hidden or expressed in hurtful ways, they can not only cause considerable damage to the relationship, but also interfere with the healing processes that you, and the survivor, must fight through. Some partners may want more physical intimacy sooner than the survivor does. Others may feel repulsed by the mere thought of it. You must allow the survivor time to come to terms with what has happened, and time to learn to separate those chaotic emotions that have bombarded him/her. They will need your support and understanding in order to become a survivor. You, however, may also need some extra support. Fortunately, in the last few years, society has developed far more resources specifically for the loved ones of a victim of sexual violence. I would certainly advise taking advantage of those opportunities. Below are some quick tips for handling this type of situation.

- Actively listen, be sincere and considerate.

- Ask open-ended questions to allow him/her to talk it out.

- Give reassurances without negating his/her feelings.

- Make sure he/she understands that the attack was not his/her fault.

- Look for opportunities to point out his/her strengths and positive aspects. You'll need to help recover his/her self-esteem and confidence. Be there, whenever you are needed.

- Suggest that he/she seek help through either a local rape crisis center or similar counseling services.

- Encourage him/her to take up a new hobby, or even join one together.

- Be aware of your limitations. Know that you cannot "cure" your partner or force decisions.

- Support his/her decisions without criticism, as

long as the decision isn't damaging or harmful to anyone.

- It's also important that you take care of yourself. Even if the victim isn't ready to talk to a hotline specialist, you can get ideas about ways to help your loved one through the recovery process.

Friends and Family of Victims

Unless you have survived some form of sexual violence, it may be very difficult for you to understand some of the feelings and emotions that accompany it. Family and friends can also experience emotional scarring, which could include wanting revenge, a desire to fix the problem, hold a belief that it wasn't that bad, or even feel emotionally disoriented. It's perfectly normal to feel scared, angry and/or confused. It may be difficult to listen to the details of the attack on someone that you love so dearly, but it's critical that you allow the victim to talk about it. Sometimes speaking aloud, in a safe atmosphere, can help a victim sort through their own confusion. There are also some people who feel that if they refuse to talk about certain feelings, then they'll eventually just go away on their own. That simply is not true! No matter the strength of the denial, or the amount of time that passes, those same fears are guaranteed to resurface again, and again. Being able to talk openly to someone they trust helps the victim put their thoughts and feelings into better perspective. If a victim is forced to hide their feelings, and/or have no one that they can talk to, then there will be an interference with the healing process for him/her, as well as for yourself. Some victims may even hide their true feelings and fears from those they know are having a hard time dealing with the assault. This is especially true for parents, spouses and children of the victim. My recognition of the struggle my father was having with the mere mention of my attack caused me to completely avoid those discussions with him. I simply didn't want to be the cause of his pain, so I kept it bottled up inside, at least until I got settled into counseling and a support group. Remember, just because someone isn't showing the emotions you would expect, it doesn't mean that they're "doing okay". Positive support is crucial, and patience is key in helping someone you love overcome these obstacles.

Many victims may feel pressured to "get over it", whether it's been a few weeks, months or even years after the attack. This pressure often comes more from the victim than from anyone else, but there are times when it can be from an overemotional or overbearing family member. Know that your reaction to this situation has an effect on how, when, and if they will recover. If you've already over reacted, know that it's never too late to come to terms with that event as long as you make sure the victim knows that you do not blame them for what happened. A heartfelt apology for an overreaction, as well as a common understanding, can be all that stands in the way of being able to move forward. Some victims may want to appear strong or not want to feel needy. They may decide not to burden family and friends with the details of the attack, thus forgetting that it will take time to recover; for the victims as much as for their friends and family. It's also best not to make the victim feel as though their taking too long to heal. Issues regarding the length of time it's taking for the victim to heal is something better handled by a therapist, counselor, doctor, etc. Below you'll find some common quick tips to help you, should this situation regrettably ever arise.

- You have to actively and openly listen to the victim, without passing judgment.

- Try to keep your emotions in check when the victim is speaking of the attack. Remember that you are there to support him/her, not the other way around.

- Make sure the victim understands that the attack was not his/her fault.

- Help empower them. Look for opportunities to point out his/her strengths and special abilities.

- Suggest calling a sexual assault hotline for guidance and support.

- Be aware of your limitations and do not force decisions.

- Don't argue with your friend, and know that he/she may direct negative feelings towards you.

- Do not compare the situation to worse one's you know of.

- Be sure to validate your friend's feelings.

- Some silence is okay. Be careful not to play a role that is not natural to you.

- Asking open-ended questions allow him/her to talk it out.

- Be there for your friend whenever he/she needs you.

- Family and friends should become a consistent support system for the victim. Be encouraging that he/she takes up a hobby of sorts.

- Be supportive of any decisions that he/she makes in attempt to recover emotionally or physically, as long as the decision isn't dangerous or harmful in anyway.

- It is also important to take care of yourself. A hotline specialist can share ways for you to help your loved one through the recovery process.

"We should not let our fears hold us back from pursuing our hopes."

~John F. Kennedy

Post Traumatic Stress Disorder

This is mostly associated with veterans of war, but can also affect victims of violent crimes. A few common effects of P.T.S.D. are avoidance, nightmares, flashbacks, panic attacks, self-harm, anxiety, depression, restlessness and/or insomnia. Some victims may become overly concerned about staying safe in situations that aren't truly dangerous. This is because traumatized people often feel like they're in danger even when they're not. They may be overly aggressive and lash out to protect themselves when there is no need.

Avoidance is a very common reaction to trauma, but it can interfere with emotional recovery and healing. Those who try to cope with trauma by avoiding thoughts and feelings about it tend to experience more severe psychological symptoms. Believe me, I attempted this as well.

Nightmares tend to involve the original horrifying set of circumstances that was involved during the attack. They can occur multiple times in a given night, or experience them very rarely. The victim may even experience the same dream repeatedly, or have different dreams with similar themes.

Self-harm is another common effect of P.T.S.D., and has a variety of meanings. Often the intention is not suicide. Self-Harm has also been referred to as 'self-mutilation', 'self-injury', self-inflicted violence', 'cutting', etc. This could be a way to punish or distract themselves, or it could be an attempt to relieve tension. It may be a way to communicate their pain. Maybe it could be an attempt to actually see evidence of injury, or as a way to nurture themselves through the process of healing the wounds. Self-Harm is not a healthy form of coping. Re-experiencing symptoms such as these are signs that the body and mind are actively struggling to cope with the traumatic experience. There are a great many therapists and counselors who are trained specifically in helping victims of P.T.S.D. successfully overcome their symptoms. Your local Rape Crisis Center will be more than happy to help you find the best support system possible.

Male Victims

As I've said before, there's no discrimination in sexual violence. Though it's suspected to actually be quite higher, statistics show that 1-in-33 men will experience some form of sexual violence in their lifetime (5). That's about the best estimate we can come to considering that sexual assault cases involving male victims are actually the least reported in the country. Most male victims are either unable or unwilling to talk about the types of things that were done to them. You wouldn't believe the number of victims who are forced into certain sexual interactions simply because they feel that they cannot stop the unwanted sexual advances. There's an immense amount of stigma surrounding male sexual violence, including that the victim will become homosexual, or that they will later become an offender themselves. Believing myths such as these can prove to be extremely dangerous, as well as damaging to victims. There are many studies that show the long term effects of sexual assault are quite damaging for either sex, but males can be more damaged by society's refusal or reluctance to accept their victimization, and by their resultant belief that they must "tough it out" in silence. Thankfully, moral support for male victims is far more accessible now than it has ever been before. I've found quite a few organizations that devote themselves to helping male victims. You'll find the contact information for each of these organizations under the Helpful Resources section in the back of this book.

Of course RAINN offers assistance for all victims, male or female, anywhere in the country. This is an organization that focuses on the victims of sexual violence as a whole rather than breaking it down to only certain types of victims.

One online organization that works specifically with male victimization is called MaleSurvivor.org, and is committed to preventing, healing, and eliminating all forms of sexual victimization of boys and men through support, treatment, research, education, advocacy, and activism.

Another extremely informative website is www.1in6.org. The mission of 1in6 is to help men who have had unwanted or abusive sexual experiences in childhood live healthier, happier lives. They also assist girlfriends, wives, partners, family members and friends by providing information and support resources through their website.

Whether you're male or female, sexual violence causes emotional distress, with some instances more severe than others. But the key thing to remember is that it was not your fault. You didn't ask for that to happen, but you can overcome it eventually. You'll need to surround yourself with only positive reinforcements, and grow some duck feathers to ward off the negative. You are strong, you will heal, and you must have faith.

> *"Nothing is more desirable than to be released from an affliction, but nothing is more frightening than to be divested of a crutch."*
>
> ~James Baldwin

Tips for Perseverance

- Now your attacker can only take what you give him. If you give him your whole life, then that's exactly what he'll take. You have the power to take back control over your life, and your emotions. Tell yourself this until you firmly believe it.

- Make a list of the things that bother you the most, leaving space between them so you can add in ways to help you overcome that issue. Each day, look for ways to help combat these problems. *(You can get some great ideas on solutions by discussing this with your counselor, therapist, advocate, social worker, etc.)*

- Set goals for yourself, whether they are daily or weekly, and decide which one(s) you want to work on first. *(This is yet another great example of what to record in your journal. Be sure to record your progression and even the lack there of. You can learn from these whether they were successful strategies or not.)*

- Create distractions for yourself once you begin feeling those torturous emotions coming over you. You MUST re-train your way of thinking. Mentally rattle off all of the ingredients for the next meal you have to cook, silently recite multiplication facts, whatever can help you refocus.

- Distractions can be a useful and necessary tactic

in allowing us to get on with day-to-day routines. Distraction is a form of avoidance, but it can be a very effective short-term coping strategy. Just keep in mind that they can become problematic when they're the primary means of coping.

- Consistency is key! You have to remain consistent and motivated to make these changes.

- Always set goals for yourself, and work towards them **consistently**.

- Remember that you have your strengths, interests, passions, desires, and hopes for the future. Try to focus your energy towards building on these.

- Take up a new hobby, sport or other activity; seriously!

- Look for a local support group that best suits your needs. You could also team up with another survivor; provided it's someone who has already moved well past the healing phase.

- Learn to appreciate a form of meditation. Relaxation techniques can decrease distress by focusing attention on disturbing feelings. There are great benefits in relaxation and breathing exercises, meditation, yoga, swimming, stretching, etc.

- Sometimes medications are necessary, but remember that they can only help you temporarily and should always be prescribed by your physician.

- Strengthening relationships with friends or family members can help you learn to reconnect with other people after a traumatic experience.

- If the attack happened in your home or neighbor-hood, consider moving. This will greatly reduce the chances of flashbacks if you're not seeing relative objects on a day-to-day basis.

- Empower yourself! Find and incorporate ways to reclaim your pride and self-esteem.

- If you fear for your safety, get a guard dog. If you've lost confidence in yourself, take some self defense classes. If you're feeling alone in this battle, join a support group. It's crucial to analyze your fears and discover methods of conquering them in order to move towards transformation.

- Be sure to read the "Self-Care for Survivors" sec-tion on the RAINN website. There is a great deal of critical information there for you and those you love. Utilizing it can help remove some of the doubt in this struggle. Be sure to get the website address in the Helpful Resources sections in the back of this book.

Self Empowerment

When a victim is struggling with the emotional trauma that follows an assault, they generally lose their sense of safety and security. There are many ways that a survivor can help empower themselves. Self defense or kickboxing classes can improve self confidence, while also providing you with a means to help protect yourself. Joining a sexual assault support group in your area can help you learn sound coping methods that have worked for others. You just have to find the right group for you. If no group is available where you live, then maybe you should consider calling the Nation Sexual Assault Hotline, where they can help connect you with a support group or other support system. There are so many different ways for you to empower yourself, you only have to find what better suits you. Personally, I like variety and learning new things. So once I feel too comfortable in one hobby, I usually try to learn a new one. I've known quite a few survivors who have stated that simply taking on new hobbies and interests have helped them tremendously in their struggle to feel a sense of self satisfaction.

One friend of mine felt so good after completing obedience training classes with her rescue dog that she decided to become a regular volunteer at a local animal rescue agency. She said that she felt her traumatic experience helped her better relate to what some of the animals there may have felt, and that providing loving comfort to animals that had also experienced some form of trauma or neglect made her feel stronger. As soon as you realize that doing something that you love is therapeutic, then you'll see tons of ways to help you empower yourself.

Through self empowerment, you are allowing yourself to find some peace and even the strength to learn to move forward. The more solid decisions that you make, the more confident you'll begin to feel about your choices. Know that you can overcome this, if only you consistently work towards healing. This is always easier when you have others supporting you through positive reinforcement.

Other Sources of Safety

Weapons

It doesn't matter whether you're for or against the use and possession of weapons, for some feel it's their only means of self-protection. If you feel it necessary to buy a weapon for self-defense, it's better not to risk failure by getting the cheapest one available. You should also consider taking a course to better understand how to use and care for any weapon. You need to know how to hold, aim and fire the weapon with confidence. If you aren't comfortable and confident with it, then you could easily fail in your attempts at self-protection. Most importantly, don't forget to get the proper permits required for the weapon of your choice. You should be able to call your local police department to inquire about local training classes for specific weapons, as well as permit requirements.

Mace or Tear Gas

These can provide an effective, temporary means of self-defense when properly used. Being that you don't have to actually touch the attacker to use mace, you have a better offensive advantage. These are most effective if you spray the chest or throat of the attacker, causing a gassy cloud to form, affecting the aggressor's eyes. However, it is usually less effective if sprayed directly into the eyes. If you don't practice with these devices in a well ventilated area, then you won't be familiar with it if the need to use it should ever arise. The down side is that these can be difficult to get to when actually needed, being typically buried in a purse or bag.

Tazer's or Stun-guns

These devices are about the size of a pocket radio or cell phone, operates on batteries, and releases an electric shock varying from 35,000 to 50,000 volts (very similar to a miniature cattle prod). Being marketed as personal protection devices primarily for women, they are specifically intended to distract an attacker rather than killing one. There are a few states, and even 2 cities, where stun guns have been outlawed. There are some states that require a permit for a private citizen to carry such a weapon. Stun guns also have their negative qualities as well. For one thing, the metal poles carrying the electrical charge must touch the attacker, so that means you would have to be in close contact for it to be effective, thus making the weapon defensive rather than offensive. They can also be difficult to get to when needed. Be sure to consider this before choosing one of these as your primary means of protection.

Watchdogs

If you're looking for security as well as companionship, then you should consider getting a dog. Even rescue dogs can teach us a lesson in dealing with certain trauma. Many of them have experienced some form of psychological or physical injury, but once in a loving environment, many of them live in the moment and seem to forget about their tragic past. Even a small dog will alert you to a stranger lurking about, giving you time to call authorities and take actions to defend yourself. It's more important that you get the right size and breed of dog for your living environment and lifestyle. Some breeds will be more territorial than others, and some will bark at every little sound they hear. If the dog will be around small children, then I would suggest getting a younger dog that can grow along with the children. If you chose a powerful breed of dog, such as a German Shepherd or Rottweiler, then you should make certain that you yourself are emotionally balanced enough to provide the proper guidance to your dog. Power breeds tend to be very protective, therefore would be quick to react if you are startled or panic. No matter the size or breed, if you provide them with a healthy, balanced environment, then you will receive their devoted loyalty.

Home Alarm Systems

Though a watchdog can do a fine job of protecting your home, a home alarm system doesn't shed or chew up your favorite pair of shoes. These devices have definitely become more popular in the last decade, but they're not exactly affordable for everyone after considering the cost of the security devices, installation and maintenance required for them to operate accordingly. Similar to insurance, you usually purchase home security systems in the hopes that you'll never actually have to use it. Even the wireless (digital) home alarm systems have their advantages and disadvantages when compared to hard-wired systems. Wireless units have a battery back up that will kick on during a power outage; however a wired alarm system will be ineffective during a power failure. Granted either of these devices will help to better protect all entrance points to your home, you should certainly do your research to find the type of system that will best suit your needs.

"Too much happens… Man performs and engenders so much more than he can or should have to bear. That's how he finds out that he can bear anything."

~William Faulkner

Crime Victim's Rights

In the last 30 years, there have been enormous advancements in the creation of legal rights for victims of crime. Today, every state has an extensive body of basic rights and protections for victims of crime within its statutory code. If you have been sexually assaulted, you should receive a Crime Victim's Bill of Rights information packet from either your local law enforcement agency or from the local rape crisis center. Victims' rights statutes have significantly influenced the manner in which victims are treated within the federal, state, and local criminal justice systems (6). Below is a list of the 9 core victims' rights as described by The National Center for Victims of Crime.

Right to Attend

Victims may have the right to attend proceedings during the criminal or juvenile justice process. The proceedings that victims may attend, such as bail hearings, trials, or parole hearings, are set by federal, state, or tribal law. Some laws may limit the trial attendance of victims who are scheduled to testify as witnesses.

Right to Compensation

Victims may have the right to be financially compensated for certain injuries or damage caused by the crime.

Compensation is a state program. Victims of federal crime or crime on tribal lands may apply for compensation in the state in which they live. Victims must file an application with the relevant compensation program and meet certain eligibility requirements.

Right to be Heard

Victims may have the right to have written or oral input during the criminal or juvenile justice process. Every state gives victims the right to submit a "victim impact statement" at sentencing. Many states also allow victims to make a statement at bail or parole hearings or to meet with the prosecutor to discuss a plea bargain.

Right to be Informed

Victims may have the right to be informed of events and proceedings in the justice process, such as trial or release of an offender from custody. Victims may also have the right to information about support services, the criminal or juvenile justice process, how to contact officials or agencies, or other matters.

Right to Protection

Victims may have the right to be protected from intimidation or harassment by the offender or others involved in the criminal or juvenile justice process. Protection may include providing a separate waiting area in court for the victim, allowing victims to seek a court order preventing the offender from contacting the victim, or prohibiting improper questioning by a lawyer.

Right to Restitution

Victims may have the right to obtain restitution, court-ordered reimbursement from offenders who have caused financial harm. Depending on the state and the crime, a court may have to order restitution in a case, or restitution may be optional. Many states also have laws about collecting restitution from the offender.

Right to Return of Property

Victims may have the right to the return of their personal property being held as evidence.

Right to a Speedy Trial

Victims may have the right to have the case resolved within a reasonable amount of time. Some states require that courts consider the interests of the victim when ruling on a request to delay, or "continue," a trial.

Right to Enforcement/Remedies of Victim

A few states give victims a way to have their rights enforced. In some states, victims may be able to file a complaint with a state agency. In others, victims may have the right to file a limited legal action.

Everyone has the legal right to defend themselves against acts of violence. However, you should also understand the laws regarding reasonable and necessary force in your state.

Generally, the doctrine of self-defense justifies the use of deadly force only to repel deadly force. The same rational for defending oneself applies when defending another person. If you honestly feel that another person is in imminent danger, then you are justified in using reasonable and necessary force to counter such a threat.

Advice for Victim Advocates

In my personal opinion, I couldn't have had a better advocate than Joye Cook, though I may be a little bias. Before retiring, she touched the lives of numerous victims, survivors, law enforcement officers, prosecutors, and especially other advocates. I felt this was the perfect place to convey some of the knowledge and experience that she shared with fellow advocates.

As an advocate, you have a significant role in helping guide victims towards becoming survivors. The first responders can have an effect on how the rape victim begins to heal, or not. It is a big responsibility, but it's one that you sign on for if you choose to be an advocate. Never tell the victim ANYTHING that you can't deliver on, just say, "I'll do my best", or "I will check into it." You lose their confidence if you promise things and then drop the ball. If you have not been sexually assaulted, don't EVER say, "I know how you feel." They will ask if it has ever happened to you. Just say, "I can only imagine how you feel" or don't say anything about how they feel. They feel like screaming, and crying, and hiding, and fighting, and balling up in a fetal position. Just let them know that you are there for them. Explain to them everything that is about to happen.

There are many ways that you can help give the victim

their control back. If you meet them at the ER, knock on the exam room door and ask permission to enter, and tell them who you are. When they give you permission to come in, don't crowd them and speak softly. Never use a tone of voice that sounds like you don't believe them, or are tired and wish you weren't there, and don't be pushy. Give them time to trust you. It helps to tell them a little about who you are, who you work for, and why you are there. Then give them an opportunity to ask you questions.

I recommend that the victim tell you the whole story before the doctor comes in and certainly before the police come for an interview. As the victim tells the story, they will remember things pushed to the back of their minds, sometimes critical information needed for either an arrest or prosecution. Joye strongly recommends that the taped interview not be given until the next day. She has often seen defense attorneys badger the victim on the stand because they didn't mention some things in the first interview, and will most certainly call them liars in the courtroom.

During the rape exam, some doctors will allow the advocate to assist the victim in retelling the story of the crime. When there has been anal penetration or oral assault, some victims are too embarrassed to tell the doctor. Sometimes they won't tell the advocate either, so it's essential for the advocate to help the victim understand how critical it is to tell everything that happened so they can be treated medically to prevent any disease or infection. It's also important that advocates have a good relationship with the hospital in their area and are familiar with the ER staff. This is always a benefit for the victim. Be sure to ask the victim if they want you to remain at the head of the table during the exam, and hold their hand. Joye says that after 23 years of working with victims, she's never found one who didn't want the advocate there during this process.

There are times when the victim will be so angry they won't be cooperative and will even yell at the advocate. You CAN NOT take offense at this... it isn't about YOU. It's about the victims feelings, they are hurt and angry, and sometimes the advocate gets the brunt of it; just don't react. Remain loving and kind... if you can't then you are in the wrong place. Almost every victim has a difficult time with the exam, and anyone touching them where the crime occurred. It is your responsibility to tell them, as the exam is taking place, what is about to happen, step-by-step. This is why it's important to know the staff of the ER; they might allow you to take the lead role, which is so important for the victim. It's also your responsibility, if the medical staff in not sensitive to the victim's needs, to take this matter up with the Director of Nursing.

The kindest thing an advocate can do for a victim of sexual violence is to explain every possible scenario that could happen during the prosecution phase, and let the victim decide whether or not to report their attack. It's always best if you can help the victim understand that reporting is so significant, even if they don't want to prosecute. At least the crime is on file when the assailant strikes another victim.

This is called a 'paper trail'. If victims are not legal adults, the crime has to be reported, by law. If the victim is well informed, then they can make a better decision on how to handle the aftermath.

During the prosecution phase, advocates should take the victim to the courtroom and familiarize them with the surroundings. Explain what will happen during the trial; give them a glossary of legal terms that will be used. Never say it is a 'slam dunk'. Even if you have fool proof evidence, a conviction is up to the jury, and sometimes juries don't convict. It is hard to get a conviction if the victim wasn't beaten. It's then a 'he said-she said' case, and the most difficult case to get a conviction. It's simply a chance you take when you go to trial.

If the case is going to trial, assist the victim in choosing her cloths and makeup for the courtroom. Defense attorneys also call attention to those dressed in low cut or short apparel, and unfortunately there are those who still think that rape could have been provoked by the victim.

Advocates should accompany the victim throughout the judicial process, and follow up for a period of time after. Sometimes the trial can bring back feelings tucked away, and start a new phase of nightmares, etc. Encourage the victim to get involved in a support group, or if you have a survivor who has gone through the process, has done well and it has been awhile, you might connect the two for support.

Note from Joye Cook:

The most rewarding aspect of being a victim advocate is meeting women like Wendy. What she has done with her life is what made my life worth while. Every time I hear her voice, my heart leaps, and my world lights up. She has left the victim behind and personifies the word SURVIVOR. I am like a Momma bear, fiercely protective, but so proud of her journey. She is using what was intended to destroy (kill) her, to help others move forward and become 'survivors' too. Wendy, I love you. ~Joye Cook

"Only a life lived for others is worth living."

~Albert Einstein

Law Enforcement and First Responders

Law enforcement officers and first responders are required to take the perspective of the victim when seeking to understand the situation and his/her response. To better relate, imagine someone asking you to stand up in public and tell of your most recent sexual experience, in very specific detail. After the initial shock you may respond, or you may tell them exactly where they can go. Your reaction could also depend on the situation, the amount of pressure you're feeling at the time, and the level of embarrassment that you may feel. You may even omit certain details or tell partial truths just to make the questioning stop. Now just imagine some people in your audience basing the validity of your claim on your personal appearance. This is starting to feel like an extremely uncomfortable and unnerving situation, don't you agree? Taking all of this into consideration can help you make sense of a victim's behavior, such as not resisting or a delay in reporting the attack.

One good way to make the victim feel that you care for her comfort is by asking if she would like a victim advocate present during the interview. Victim advocates are trained to provide the necessary moral support without being disruptive to the investigative process. Most advocates would even suggest that the victim make contact with a victim advocate before having an officer tape the official interview. This is mainly because the advocate can help the victim prepare for what she is about to experience, thus giving you an interview that could have less misdirection and be much easier for you to understand. The interview process can be very stressful when the victim is required to specifically detail everything that was done to them, and then consider the level of embarrassment that they'll certainly feel. There are some victims that may feel intimidated by the presence of a male officer, especially uniformed and armed, following an assault. On the other hand, some may feel safer in the presence on a male officer. Given the suspect is likely male, the positive contact with a man after the assault can be an important factor towards the recovery for some victims. Pay close attention to her reactions and many times you will be able to tell what can/will trigger a fear. First responders are also in the position to help the victim regain some of the lost control by asking where she would like to sit, or if you could call someone for her, or have someone bring her a change of clothes if evidence is to be collected from her person. Asking these types of questions will certainly help her feel that you are concerned about her well-being while also helping to felicitate a good rapport.

Every law enforcement officer should be familiar with recent laws and victims rights. If there is no Victim Assistance Coordinator or Advocate within your department, then it is your responsibility to provide this information to the victim by providing them a Victims Rights Packet. In most states, the victim must receive this information packet within 72 hours of the crime being reported. This helps to protect the officer and the department from certain liabilities, while also informing the victim as to the types of resources that may be available to them. There's a lot to consider when responding to victims of sexual violence. Below are a few quick tips that you may want to keep in mind.

<u>DO</u>:

- Apply psychological first-aid by maintaining a calm, reassuring voice and communicating empathy. Create an open and nonjudgmental demeanor.

- Be respectful, tactful and pay close attention to details. Even a victim that's in a traumatic state can sense uncertainty.

- Respect personal space. It may not be a good idea to touch the victim immediately following an assault. Some victims may even flinch at a pat on the shoulder.

- Understand the victims need to feel safe. By reassuring her that she is "now" safe, the word "now" helps bring back current reality that the assault is over.

- Hide your skepticism. Even though you're basically programmed to be skeptical, disbelief is one the greatest fears for victims; especially if there's little or no evidence.

- Always think before you speak and try reflective listening.

- Suggest that she begin keeping a journal. This will

help with recording memories, help prepare for the trial, and even assist in the healing process.

- If the victim becomes too upset, take a break. Deescalate the situation before you continue.

- Allow the victim to vent emotions.

- Skip questions that the victim has trouble remembering. Make note of it and go back to it later. Latter questions may even jar her memory. As comfort levels increase, some questions will be a little easier to answer.

- Disorganized thinking patterns are quite normal for victims, especially if they are in a state of shock. Remember that the victim's own discomfort or shame could cause some inconsistencies.

DON'T:

- Promise a certain outcome. The victim may inadvertently blame you if there's a different one.

- Say "it could have been worse". In the mind of the victim, there isn't much that could be worse than having your own mind and body so violated.

- Interrupt the victim too frequently. She may think you aren't taking her seriously.

- Show frustration. If she feels too much pressure, she may clam up or withdraw altogether out of her own frustration.

- Ask for unnecessary sexual details. Asking the necessary questions is uncomfortable enough without having to also answer those that are not pertinent.

- Act in an unprofessional manner.

When the time comes for pictures to be taken of evidence or the crime scene, be sure that you get clear and focused pictures. Pay attention to the lighting and various angles. These pictures are many times used in court, as well as parole hearings. Remember the saying "a picture is worth a thousand words"? This is especially true in crime photos.

Keep the victim informed using "we" statements. The word "we" provides the victim with a sense that this is a team effort and helps provide a sense of control. (Example, "We are going to talk about the incident", or "We need to review this information together")

If you need her assistance, be sure to use "I" statements. (Example, "I would like your help with my report for better accuracy", or "I've talked to many victims who've had the same concerns as you".) This will help the victim understand that her complaint is being taken seriously and handled professionally.

Response to Victims with Disabilities

It's important to know that federal law requires, with few exceptions, that law enforcement officials make reasonable modifications to policies, practices, and procedures where needed to accommodate crime victims who have disabilities. People who have disabilities can be far more vulnerable to victimization than others in society. Many are less able to recognize and avoid danger. They're also less likely to report a violation to law enforcement, much less assist in an investigation. This is primarily due to the fact that they're often abused and/or assaulted by their own care givers. This creates a fear that if they tell someone, then who would care for them. There are many things that you can do to help your investigation, while also helping the victim of a disability. No matter the condition, never show any of your own frustrations. Below are some things to keep in mind when it comes to working with victims of sexual violence that also have various impairments.

<u>Alzheimer's Disease</u>

- Approach the victim from the front and maintain eye contact.

- Remember their impaired short term memory.

- Never leave the victim alone; they could stray or wander off.

- Ask one question at a time, and be patient waiting for the answers.

- Give simplified step-by-step instructions during the interview.

- Expect difficulties in making yourself understood.

Mental Illness

- Keep interview simple and brief.

- Avoid sudden movements, whispering, continuous eye contact, forced conversations, obvious impatience, arguments and touching.

- Remember that hallucinations are frighteningly real to these victims. Acknowledge paranoia and delusions by empathizing with their feelings, without agreeing or disagreeing with them. Try reassuring them that the hallucinations will not harm them if they calm down.

Other Mental Impairments

- Break from interview every 15 minutes or so.

- Remember that the victim may be eager to please.

- Try to let the victim lead the interview.

- Avoid 'yes' or 'no' questions.

- Allow at least 30 seconds for the victim to understand and answer each question.

- Keep your terminology as simple as possible.

Blind or Visually Impaired

- Tell the victim your name, badge number and the phone number to reach your dispatcher when responding to victims who are alone. Encourage them to call and verify your identity.

- Keep the victim informed when you or someone with you is stepping away from the conversation.

- When escorting, offer your arm rather than holding the arm of the victim. Orient the victim to their surroundings and give clues as to what lies ahead when guiding them.

Deaf or Hearing Impaired

- Victims may not be literate in written English, but may know American Sign Language (ASL).

- Avoid making jokes thinking that the victim cannot hear you. Some read lips extremely well.

- Always face the victim so that your eyes and mouth are clearly visible. Avoid looking away or at your notes while speaking.

- Speak directly to the victim, not the interpreter.

- Speak clearly and be prepared to repeat yourself.

- Never use a child to communicate with an adult victim.

"Great works are performed not by strength, but by perseverance."

~ Samuel Johnson

About Sexual Predators

In this section, I will be referring to sexual predators in general terms of "he". As I've explained before, there is no discrimination in sexual violence. Sexual predators belong to both sexes, but are more commonly men. For the simple reason of making this easier to follow, I will be referring to the offender as "he" and the victim as "she", but this is most certainly not always the situation in real cases. The victim could just as easily be male, and the attacker a female or another male.

There are no definite physical features to give away a sexual predator. You won't find a label across their foreheads saying "DANGER: RAPIST!" In fact, many look just as normal as your uncle, cousin or neighbor. And throughout history we've been trying to figure out what exactly we're supposed to do with them. There's an article called "The Civil Commitment of Sex Offenders" by Harold Zonana, that explains, "Between 1930 and 1960, a number of states passed "sexual psychopath laws" that offered indefinite hospitalization and treatment in lieu of incarceration for offenders who committed repetitive sexual crimes. When treatment was not sufficiently effective, and when retribution became a more primary goal than rehabilitation, these statutes were repealed or fell into disuse (2)." This lead me to

wonder about our progression of such treatment. Some psy-
chologist believe that they can rectify the offender's deviate
behavior through various forms of therapy, but many others
in the psychology field believe that it's virtually impossible
to rehabilitate such behaviors. If it can be clearly verified that
rehabilitation isn't possible, then maybe we need to rethink
that idea of indefinite commitment. If such terrorizing behavior can't be changed, then the primary goal should then
be to better protect society from them. If each state had a
specific facility exclusively for recurring sex offenders, then
they wouldn't crowd the prison systems either, right? Well
I've learned of a few states that have started thinking along
those very lines. State facilities that specialize in the treatment and containment of repeat sex offenders can prove
to have a few different benefits, but it would also cost the
equivalent of building and operating a new prison facility.
Many states claim not to have the funds for that. Personally,
I think it would be more like an investment in security that
should be seriously considered.

It's suggested that the vast majority of rapists have no
mental disorders other than antisocial personality disorder,
though many offenders meet diagnostic criteria for pedophilia, and may also suffer from various forms of anxiety,
depression, or psychotic disorders (2). Even thought there
have been multiple attempts at various types of treatment
programs for sexual offenders, there have been many debates
on whether or not they are actually effective. One of the
most difficult issues in the treatment of sex offenders is how

to measure improvement. Not to mention the fact that many sex offenders plea guilty to lesser charges of crimes that are not sexual offenses, thus not required to complete a treatment program for sex offenders. As far as the effectiveness of such programs, most have failed to provide any credible evidence that treatment is effective in reducing relapse of sexual offenses (3).

Many sexual predators tend to have either a low self esteem, or have some control issues. They often find a pattern of behavior that they stick to. Most rapists are serial rapists, repeatedly offending until eventually being caught and stopped. Most commonly, sexual offenders are middle-class, well educated, successful, Caucasian men.

From the different studies that I've read, it's generally agreed that there are 3-4 specific types of rapists, varying in degrees of intensity. The **first** type is generally the least violent of these four. He probably acts the perfect gentleman, charming and witty, thus making himself seem a less likely threat. He's all about power reassurance, while getting exactly what he wants. He may apologize for his actions or express concern for what you're feeling during, or following, the attack. This type is the standard date rapist, and most likely the most common type. The **second** type is more power assertive, even somewhat edgy about having things a certain way. This type will be more aggressive in their actions, and you may be able to see them struggle with inner conflicts (almost like split personalities). This type also tends to objectify women, seeing them more as an object to conquer. The most important thing to remember about this type is that they can be somewhat unpredictable in their behavior and actions. The **third** type is far more retaliatory and violent in actions, may enjoy seeing your fear, and feel that he has every right to do what ever he wishes. He frequently thinks in terms of revenge, whether his reasons are real or imagined. A few different studies considered this type to be too closely related to the fourth type to separate them. But the studies that felt otherwise explain the **forth** type as the most severe, with a tenancy to be motivated by violence and domination at their own hand. This type usually experiences a form of excitement through his own sadistic actions. They are typically quite intelligent, and constantly look for opportunities. Often times they do intend to kill, and will plan extensively with that goal in mind. It's also said that this type commonly feels the need to go to different extremes/severity just to get a higher rush, (much like drugs; the more you use, the more you need to get that equal high/rush). Many people feel that this type will never stop, and will progressively get more severe in their actions as they repeat the offense.

Most importantly, all of these types can pretend to be quite normal, and can be very good conversationalists. They may inquire about something of interest to you. They may even find some way of being helpful in order to break the ice. And it's quite easy sometimes to dismiss your immediate concerns as paranoia or an overactive imagination. If you begin to get a gut feeling that something may not be right about a stranger, then get away from them at once! It's better to be wrong and safe than to be right and too late.

Typically there are certain patterns to the behaviors of sexual predators when they consider potential victims. Some are simply opportunists who look for someone who is just in the wrong place at the wrong time, but many commit to a certain sequence of steps that they faithfully stick to. The first step is generally target selection. Many often like the perception of the victim being flattered by his attention. Any vulnerability on her part would cause her to be seen as easy prey, just as my attacker saw vulnerability in not only my drinking, but also my crying after the argument with my boyfriend. Then there's the approach or evaluation stage. At this phase, the offender is usually quite flattering and very attentive; maybe he even desensitizes himself to any intrusions. He may push alcohol or drugs, thinking of them as tools that reduce reluctance and/or slow the victim's reaction time. My attacker watched me cry and waited until he overheard someone urging me to go for a walk to calm down. Then he approached, he listened, encouraged me to drink more. Generally, the offender will then move on to the separation stage, when he will try to get her away from other people, where they can be alone. Just as my attacker volunteered to walk with me, and later urged me to walk further (for his own comfort). It's suggested that more than half of this type will try to take the victim back to his place, simply because it's within his comfort zone, but most find another secluded spot nearby. Then they will usually make an attempt at consensual sex. Sometimes when the victim agrees, the sequence will stop and he may begin to behave normally. However, if the victim rejects his advances, then he'll become more aggressive, and the sequence continues. Rejection was what triggered the violence and rage in my attacker. Then they usually move on to intimidation. You would definitely notice a radical behavior change, showing far more aggression now than before. His goal would be to make the victim believe that she won't be able to leave until she complies. He may force you to beg, but then punish you for being so weak. The form of intimidation that my attacker used was the multiple blows to my face, leading to him dragging me into the woods by my hair. This Neanderthal type behavior made him feel powerful and in complete control. Typically, this is followed by the sexual violation stage. His actions are usually intended to be insulting and degrading. He may even drag this stage out as long as he can imagine more ways to accomplish his goal of domination and humiliation, at least for as long as he feels safe. Then many go through the termination phase. He doesn't want her to tell anyone about the attack. He may even attempt to make her feel guilty for what happened, as though she were responsible.

One thing you should definitely realize is that many sexual predators love to go to the hot new clubs or bars in town and just watch the other people there. Sometimes they see an opportunity, and they usually act on it. If you are in a social situation, do not accept drinks from strangers;

especially if you didn't see it go from the bartender's hands to yours. It's pretty commonly known that there are various types of drugs that can be dissolved into a drink, are odorless and tasteless, and can incapacitate a person. This would leave you completely vulnerable if you aren't around a person that you know you can trust. It doesn't matter if they're male or female, if you don't know them very well, or not at all, then they could have other motives. The effects of such drugs do vary, but some could have effects that last for several hours, particularly if mixed with alcohol. Sometimes a person can simply wake the next morning feeling mentally clouded and just know that something isn't right. Should that ever happen to you, make sure that you see your physician **very** soon after, prior to cleaning yourself! Many of these drugs can be detected through tests, and you should make sure that you're treated to prevent certain diseases or pregnancy.

I do remember reading somewhere that many sexual offenders declared that physically hurting someone wasn't as exciting, because that type of pain goes away too easily. Many preferred to hurt someone emotionally, which often stays with a person far longer. What the survivor needs to remember is that as long as they're alive, they can overcome just about anything.

What Sexual Predators Look For

I've spent a lot of time perusing research about what inspires sexual offenders, and even reading interviews of incarcerated sexual predators on what they look for in potential victims. There are some very interesting things that I noticed and I feel are extremely important for everyone to consider.

- The first that thing many looked for was hairstyle. They seemed to prefer someone with a ponytail, bun, braid or other hairstyle that can easily be grabbed.

- Clothing is another consideration to sexual predators, though not a major obstacle. They prefer clothing that is easily removable, but many also admit to carrying scissors with them specifically to cut the fabric.

- Quite a few admitted that they prefer women who are on their cell phones, searching through their bags or distracted by other activities while walking. This usually means that their guard is down and they can be easily overpowered.

- The top three places women are abducted are from grocery store parking lots, office parking lots or garages, and public restrooms.

- The thing these predators are looking for most is

to grab a victim and quickly move her to a second location where he doesn't have to worry so much about getting caught.

- Only 2% of predators interviewed admitted that they carried weapons because in most areas rape carries a less sentence than rape with a weapon does.

- Many of the offenders acknowledged that if the victim put up a good fight, they got discouraged because it only takes a minute or two to realize that a victim who is fighting back is going to be time consuming.

Helpful Resources

www.justyellfire.com
Dallas Jessup, Founder and Spokesperson, demonstrates her mission to make every girl between the ages of 11-19 aware of self-defense techniques that could prevent an attack.

www.rainn.org
Rape, Abuse and Incest National Network, (RAINN), is the nation's largest anti-sexual assault organization and operates the National Sexual Assault Hotline, offering free, confidential counseling, 24 hours a day: *1-800-656-HOPE*.

www.tkastnd.org
Take A Stand Against Violence provides a safe and secure environment for survivors of sexual assault and domestic violence through online moral support, victim advocacy, and community education. Through these mediums they hope to help victims as well as survivors gather their strength and regain control.

www.malesurvivor.org
Commitment to preventing, healing, and eliminating all forms of sexual victimization of boys and men through

support, treatment, research, education, advocacy, and activism.

www.1in6.org

Their mission is to help men who have had unwanted or abusive sexual experiences in childhood live healthier, happier lives. They also help girlfriends, wives, partners, family members and friends by providing information and support resources on the web.

www.victimrights.org

Founded as the first law center in the nation dedicated solely to serving the legal needs of sexual assault victims, the Victim Rights Law Center is the leader in representing sexual assault victims' legal rights within the civil context. Not only providing legal representation to victims of rape and sexual assault to help rebuild their lives, but also promote a national movement committed to seeking justice for every rape and sexual assault victim.

www.nsvrc.org

The National Sexual Violence Resource Center. If you're looking for more useful information about sexual violence, this is a wonderful organization. They list helpful resources available nationwide.

Legal Term Definitions

Accessory – a person who aids or contributes to a crime as a subordinate. An accessory performs acts that aid others in committing a crime or in avoiding apprehension.

Accusation – a charge of wrong doing against a person, thus institute legal proceedings charging someone with a crime.

Advocacy – the active taking up of a legal cause.

Affidavit – a written statement made under oath before an officer of the court, a notary public or other person legally authorized to certify the statement.

Alias - "otherwise known as"; an indication that a person is known by more than one name.

Alibi – an excuse that prove the physical impossibility that a suspected person could have committed the crime.

Appeal – the request to a higher court to review and reverse the decision of a lower court.

Arraignment – an initial step in the criminal process in which a defendant is formally charged with an offense, given a copy of the complaint, indictment, information, or other accusatory instrument, and informed of his constitutional rights, including the pleas he wishes to enter.

Arrest – To seize or capture; to take or hold a suspected ʾcriminal with legal authority, as by a law enforcement officer.

Bail – a monetary or other security given to secure the release of the defendant until time of trial and to assure his appearance at every stage of the proceedings.

Carnal Knowledge – sexual intercourse; the slightest penetration of the female sexual organ by the male sexual organ; does not require rupture of the hymen.

Civil – the branch of law that pertains to suits other than criminal practice and is concerned with the rights of the people involved.

Coercion - any form of compulsion or constraint that compels or induces a person to act otherwise than freely.

Concurrent – existing together; in conjunction with.

Corroborating Evidence – evidence complimentary to evidence already given and tending to strengthen or confirm it; additional evidence of a different character on the same point.

Cross Examination – the questioning of a witness, by a lawyer other than the one who called the witness.

Date Rape - forcible sexual intercourse by a male acquaintance of a female, during a voluntary social engagement in which the woman did not intend to submit to the sexual advances and resisted the acts by verbal refusals, denials or pleas to stop, and/or physical resistance.

Defendant – In civil proceedings, the party responding to the complainant; one who is sued and called upon to make satisfaction for a wrong complained of by another. In criminal proceedings, the accused.

Degree of Crime – a measure of the seriousness of a criminal act that determines the range of criminal sanctions that may be imposed for the crime.

Direct Examination – the initial questioning of a witness by the party who called the witness.

DNA Testing – scientific evidence used in criminal cases and in paternity suits.

Facilitation – in criminal law, a statutory offense rendering a person guilty when, believing it probable that he or she is someone who intends to commit a crime, he or she assists the criminal in obtaining the means to commit the crime, and in fact such conduct does aid the person to commit the crime.

Felony – A generic term employed to distinguish high crimes from minor offenses known as misdemeanors; crimes declared to be such by statute or to be 'true crimes' by the common law.

Force – physical acts or the threat of physical acts intentionally used to do an act or to commit a crime.

Guardian Ad Litem – a person appointed by the court to protect the interests of a ward in a legal proceeding.

Implied Consent – consent that is found to exist solely

because certain actions or signs would lead a reasonable person to believe that consent is present, whether or not that consent is even specifically expressed; in criminal law, generally used as a defense against rape, whereby the defendant claims that he acted under a reasonable and honest belief based on the fact that the woman consented to his advance.

Incest – a criminal offense of sexual intercourse between members of a family, or those between whom marriage would be illegal because of blood relationship.

Indictment – a formal written accusation, drawn up and submitted under oath to a grand jury by the public prosecuting attorney, charging one or more persons with a crime.

Informer - one who, on a confidential basis, gives information about some wrongdoing to the police.

Jurisdiction – the geographic or political entity governed by a particular legal system or body of laws.

Jury – a group, composed of the peers of the parties or a cross section of the community, summoned and sworn to decide on the facts in issue at a trial.

Kidnapping – Unlawful carrying away of a person against his or her will; false imprisonment coupled with removal of the victim to another place. This is a serious felony in the United States.

Lewdness – criminal act of sexual indecency committed in public.

Lineup – the police procedure in which a person suspected of a crime is placed in a line with several other persons and a witness to the crime attempts to identify the suspect as the person who committed the crime.

Misdemeanor – A class of criminal offenses less serious than felonies and sanctioned by less severe penalties.

Modus Operandi - A Latin term; a manner of operation. The means of accomplishing an act; especially characteristic method employed by the defendant in repeated criminal acts.

Molestation - the crime of sexual acts with children up to the age of 18, including touching of private parts, exposure of genitalia, taking of pornographic pictures, rape, inducement of sexual acts with the molester or with other children and variations of these acts by pedophiles. This also applies to incest by a relative with a minor family member and any unwanted sexual acts with adults short of rape.

Motion – an application to the court requesting an order in favor of the applicant.

Next Friend - a competent person who, although not an appointed guardian, acts in behalf of a party who is unable to look after his or her own interests or manage his or her own lawsuit. Although not considered a party to the suit, but rather regarded as an agent of the court to protect the rights of the disabled person.

Oath – an affirmation of the truth of a statement.

Parole – in criminal law, a conditional release from

imprisonment that entitles the person receiving it to serve the remainder of his or her term outside prison if he or she complies with all the conditions connected with his or her release.

Pedophilia - an obsession with children as sex objects. Overt acts, including taking sexually explicit photographs, molesting children and exposing one's genitalia to children, are all crimes.

Perjury – criminal offense of making false statements under oath.

Plea Bargaining – the process whereby the accused and the prosecutor negotiate a mutually satisfactory disposition of a case.

Rape – the act of unlawful sexual intercourse accomplished through force or threat of force by one party and implying lack of consent and resistance from the other party.

Rape Crisis Counselor Privilege – privilege against disclosure of records and notes afforded by some states to professionals who give victims of sexual assault counseling and emotional support. The privilege is usually available in both civil and criminal proceedings. In jurisdictions where it has been adopted, its availability represents a judgment that the confidentiality of a rape victim and a rape crisis counselor is sufficiently important to justify limiting the right of the criminal defendant to confront the witness against him or her under the Sixth Amendment.

Rape Shield Laws – laws that limit the questions a defendant may ask about the lifestyle of the victim unless those questions can be shown to be essential for a fair trial.

Redirect Examination – the questioning of a witness by a party who called the witness, which occurs after the witness has been subjected to cross examination.

Registration of Offenders – statute requiring lifetime registration of convicted sex offenders (including those found not guilty by reason of insanity) with law enforcement, and allowing law enforcement to notify the community of the sex offenders known address and vehicle. Federally, in many states, such a statute is called Megan's Law.

Self Defense – the self protection of ones person, or preservation of members of ones family, and , to a lesser extent, ones property, from harm by an aggressor, in a way and under circumstances that the law recognizes as justifying the protective measures.

Sex Offender - a person convicted of a sexual offense such as rape/sexual assault, sexual contact or lewdness. Some states house sex offenders together and offer specialized counseling programs

Stalking – persistent, distressing, or threatening behavior consisting of at least two elements: the actor must repeatedly follow the victim and must engage in conduct that annoys or alarms the victim and serves no legitimate purpose.

Statement – a declaration of fact; an allegation by a witness.

Statute – an act of legislature, adopted under its

constitutional authority, by prescribed means and in certain form, so that it becomes the law governing conduct within its scope.

Statutory Rape - sexual intercourse with a female below the legal age of consent but above the age of a child, even if the female gave her consent, did not resist and/or mutually participated. In all but three states the age of consent is 18, and the age above which the female is no longer a child varies, although age 14 is common.

Subpoena - a Latin term meaning 'under penalty'. A writ issued under authority of a court to compel the appearance of a witness at a judicial proceeding; disobedience may be punishable as 'contempt of court'.

Testify – the making of a statement under oath, usually related to a judicial proceeding; to make a solemn declaration under oath or affirmation for the purpose of establishing proof of some fact to the court.

Venue - the proper or most convenient location for trial of a case. Normally, the venue in a criminal case is the judicial district or county where the crime was committed. For civil cases, venue is usually the district or county which is the residence of a principal defendant, where a contract was executed or is to be performed, or where an accident took place. However, the parties may agree to a different venue for convenience (such as where most witnesses are located).

Verdict - the opinion rendered by a jury, or a judge when there is no jury, on a question of fact. A verdict differs from a judgment in that a verdict is not a judicial determination, but rather a finding of fact that the trial court may accept or reject and utilize in formulating its judgment.

Writ – a legal order issued by the authority and in the name of the state to compel a person to do something therein mentioned.

References

1. Kolivas, E. D., Gross, A. M. Assessing sexual aggression: Addressing the gap between rape victimization and perpetration prevalence rates. Aggression and Violent Behavior (2006), doi:10.1016/j.avb.2006.10.002

2. Zonana H: The civil commitment of sex offenders. Science 278:1248-1249, 1997

3. Furby L, Weinrott MR, Blackshaw L: Sex offender recidivism: a review. Psychological Bulletin 105:3-30, 1989[Medline]

4. www.fbi.gov/publications/leb/2010/may2010/violence_feature.htm Sabrina Garcia and Margaret Henderson, "Blind Reporting of Sexual Violence," *FBI Law Enforcement Bulletin*, June 1999, 12-16.

5. www.rainn.org
   Rape, Abuse, and Incest National Network, National Sexual Assault Hotline

6. www.ncvc.org
   DNA and Crime Victims: What Victims Need to Know. The National Center for Victims of Crime. 2008.

7. www.ovw.usdoj.gov
   Anonymous Reporting and Forensic Examinations.

Department of Justice: Office on Violence Against Women. 2008.

8. Gifis, Steven H.
   Dictionary of Legal Terms: a simplified guide to the language of law / by Steven H. Gifis.-3rd ed.

9. www.nsvrc.org
   National Sexual Violence Resource Center

10. Sawyer, R. G., Pinciaro, P. J., & Jessell, J. K. (1998). Effects of coercion and verbal consent on university students' perception of date rape. American Journal of Health Behavior, 22, 46–53.